When ONLY a MIRACLE Will Do!

By Marilyn Hickey

Marilyn
Hickey
Ministries

P.O. Box 17340 • Denver, Colorado 80217

Contents

Chapter One

HOW TO RECEIVE A MIRACLE

Today is a day of miracles. More than ever before, God is pouring out His grace and mercy on His people and showing us that miracles are ready and available just for the asking! God wants to turn our hopeless situations into miraculous turnarounds. But in order to get our miracles, we must know just how to receive our miracles.

THE MAKING
OF A MIRACLE

All miracles have a starting place. Usually miracles begin when all of our human efforts have failed, and the situation still looks absolutely hopeless. But hopeless situations do not make God helpless, and we see proof of this in II Kings 3.

The story involves two kings: one named Jehoram and the other named Jehoshaphat. Jehoram, the king of Israel, was an evil man, and the ten tribes under his rule were filled with ungodly men. But Jehoshaphat, the king of Judah, was a godly man, and his two tribes served God with all their might.

Now there was a custom in Israel that had been going on for over 150 years:

And Mesha king of Moab was a sheep-master, and rendered unto the king of Israel an hundred thousand lambs, and

3

an hundred thousand rams, with the wool (II Kings 3:4).

When David was king, he conquered Moab. The Moabites then became David's servants and brought him gifts (see II Samuel 8:2). Since then, the Moabites paid tribute to the king of Israel.

Balaam had been hired by the king of Moab to go and curse the Israelites. But Balaam was unable to curse what God had blessed. The word of the Lord came to Balaam, and he prophesied that Moab would have to pay tribute to Israel as a means of blessing. When David became the king of Israel, the prophecy was fulfilled, and wicked, ungodly Moab was required to send Israel thousands of sheep and goats yearly to fulfill the tribute.

So far, all the past kings of Moab had not complained about the deal. But one morning Mesha, the king of Moab, woke up with a bad attitude. He was disgusted with having to pay that tribute every year. So he sent a message to Jehoram that said, "Listen here, I'm tired of giving you all those sheep and goats every year and I'm not going to do it anymore."

You can imagine how Jehoram felt after hearing Mesha's words. Those sheep and goats were worth thousands and thousands of dollars to Israel's economy. It was money in their pocket,

4

and now they weren't going to get any at all. Jehoram was simply sick. He had to find a way to get the king of Moab to pay the tribute so that Israel would not be in financial trouble:

> *And he went and sent to Jehoshaphat the king of Judah, saying, The king of Moab hath rebelled against me: wilt thou go with me against Moab to battle? And he said, I will go up: I am as thou art, my people as thy people, and my horses as thy horses* (II Kings 3:7).

Now we know that Jehoram was a wicked man. First of all, he came from a bad family. His father was the wicked King Ahab and his mother the horrible Jezebel. Jehoram worshipped idols and led his country away from the living God. But Jehoshaphat was a godly man and king. He chose to serve God and to lead his country in righteousness.

We see here that Jehoshaphat was not being very smart. He knew that Jehoram had ungodly principles and was not a righteous man. Jehoshaphat should have said, "Hey Jehoram, I realize now you are in a tough spot here, but I can't compromise my values to go and do battle with you. I serve the living God, and this is not God's best plan for me." But instead, Jehoshaphat said he'd be glad to help. He didn't even think twice about helping Jehoram or that doing so would

5

compromise his faith.

Sometimes we make bad compromises with the world also. We think that we can step off into the world now and then and not get dirty. "Oh, I know I am a Christian but just this one time won't hurt." But God doesn't want us to get off into junk and trash. He wants us to walk in His Word so that we can be blessed and protected. Jehoshaphat, in his desire for peace, didn't really do what God wanted him to do; and serious trouble was inevitable. And because trouble was coming, a miracle was in the making.

THE IMMEDIACY OF A MIRACLE

So Jehoram made an alliance with Jehoshaphat and also with the king of Edom. Together the three kings made plans to battle Moab. When their plans were finished, they began their journey:

> *So the king of Israel went, and the king of Judah, and the king of Edom: and they fetched a compass of seven days' journey: and there was no water for the host, and for the cattle that followed them* (II Kings 3:9).

Oh no, problem number one had already arisen; and, it was a big, big problem. The three kings and their armies had traveled for seven days, and the seven days had been full of walking, walking, and more walking. Cattle had been brought along for food, and they were tired and grumpy too. But the real problem here wasn't tired feet or hungry men and cattle; it was that there was no water—and everyone was very thirsty.

By this point King Jehoram's attitude was not very good. The men and cattle were in desperate trouble, and there didn't seem to be any hope:

> *And the king of Israel said, Alas! that the LORD hath called these three kings together, to deliver them into the hand of Moab!* (II Kings 3:10).

Jehoram was not a happy man. He needed a miracle, but he didn't know how to get one. His golden idols were back home and he knew they wouldn't come to the rescue. He didn't have a relationship with God and so all he could think was that God must hate him and want him to die of thirst. At this point, Jehoram's outlook was not too good.

When we get into serious problems, sometimes we act just like Jehoram. We think that all these hardships must be happening because we've blown it, and God is mad at us. But that is just the devil whispering in our ears and feeding us lies. God doesn't ever turn His back on us and say, "Ok, I'm going to give you this trial and then leave you high and dry; hopefully this will teach you how to be spiritual!" God is a good God and He doesn't leave you "dry as a bone" in your time of need. Rather He makes you "*. . . as a tree planted by the waters, . . .*" (Jeremiah 17:8), growing and flourishing with life!

This whole situation could have turned into a total disaster. But Jehoshaphat knew that his God was a God of great miracles. He knew that God could bring them a miracle for their time of need. So, instead of giving up, Jehoshaphat said:

> *. . . Is there not here a prophet of the LORD, that we may enquire of the LORD by him? And one of the king of Israel's servants answered and said, Here is Elisha . . . . And Jehoshaphat said, The word of the LORD is with him. So the king of Israel and Jehoshaphat and the king of Edom went down to him* (II Kings 3:11,12).

Jehoshaphat did the smart thing. He didn't whine and moan and groan about the problem. Nor did he say to himself, "Well, I really blew it by compromising with Jehoram. God probably is mad at me, and He won't do anything for me, so forget the miracle." Jehoshaphat looked to God for help because he knew that God was forgiving and understanding. He just knew that God could help them if they would simply ask.

A few years ago I was in a situation that could

have robbed me of my faith and made me unable to believe for a miracle. We had invited Pat Boone to come and speak here in Denver. I had such positive feelings about this meeting and so wanted it to be successful. But instead of the meeting being a success, it turned out to be a total disaster! Everything that could have gone wrong went wrong. The water main broke, the electricity went off, the person at the book table was robbed, and many other things backfired as well.

Well, as you can imagine, I didn't feel too spiritual when I went in to work the next morning. Just as I walked past my secretary, she reminded me that I had a speaking engagement that morning at 11:30. Immediately I was angry because I felt so out of it and didn't feel like ministering. But I had to go and I couldn't back out of it.

I called several friends and asked them if they could go with me and pray for me while I was speaking. But no one could go, and I just got more and more upset. I had no friends who could go with me, I had no idea where the place was located, and I had to be there by 11:30. Plus, everything had fallen apart the day before, and I was really out of it.

Well, I managed to arrive at the place on time. I got out of the van and someone came to me and said, "What are you doing here at 11:30? You're not due till 1:00!" Oh, I was furious! I asked if there was a place I could go and pray until the meeting started. I went into the classroom and murmured a little, but I tried to repent a little too.

At one o'clock I went into the sanctuary to speak. No sooner had I started to speak when something cracked—it sounded like glass. In the back room I saw a woman crying, and her friend stood up beside her and said, "We had a miracle. This woman had a fused spine, and she couldn't move her head. But that 'pop' was her spine; she can move her head. God has done a miracle!" In addition to that miracle, many more people were saved, healed, and baptized in the Holy Spirit.

Needless to say, I was curious as to why the meeting had gone so well when I felt so out of it. The Lord answered me and said, "Yes, but I'm so in it!"

Like Jehoshaphat, I felt I had really blown it; I didn't feel spiritual at all. But God immediately gave me a miracle for my crisis situation. And as we will soon see, God gives miracles to those who serve Him with all their heart and soul— sometimes, even when they have blown it!

RECEIVING
A MIRACLE

So the three kings went to Elisha and asked for a word from the Lord. After Elisha heard their request, he said:

> . . . *As the LORD of hosts liveth, before whom I stand, surely, were it not that I regard the presence of Jehoshaphat the king of Judah, I would not look toward thee, nor see thee* (II Kings 3:14).

God doesn't mince any words here. He bluntly says that if it wasn't for Jehoshaphat being a godly man and king, He wouldn't even turn an ear to hear the plea for help. In other words, God wasn't interested in Jehoram's business because Jehoram wasn't interested in God's business!

You see, God is very particular about miracle giving. Queen Jezebel, with all of her wicked and vile ways, probably never received a miracle from God. Why? Because Jezebel wasn't in the habit of receiving from God—in fact, she loved idols and *hated God!*

God wants to be the gift-giver of miracles. The devil may come and slap you around and make things look impossible. You may think that God could never, ever patch up that mess. But I have good news for you! Miracles are one of God's specialities! No situation is ever beyond God's loving and caring hand. Christians are in the market to receive miracles because of God's endless grace toward us.

Now Elisha knew that God's favor was in the circumstance; and, therefore, prayer was the next

11

step. Elisha wanted to be absolutely sure that God's voice was heard. But before Elisha prayed, he asked for a minstrel to come and play worshipful music to the Lord:

> *But now bring me a minstrel. And it came to pass, when the minstrel played, that the hand of the LORD came upon him* (II Kings 3:15).

In an attitude of worship and prayer, Elisha asked God what should be done for the three kings. A miracle was needed, and Elisha wanted God's best. Notice that Elisha didn't panic and hurry to get an answer from the Lord. He didn't say, "Oh God, You've got a very big problem here and You'd better hurry!" Rather, he waited on God by worshiping Him and prayerfully seeking Him. Elisha knew that for the sake of one righteous man God would send a life-saving miracle.

ACCOMPLISHING A MIRACLE

Elisha had heard the word from the Lord. In order to accomplish a miracle, hard work was necessary:

> *. . . Thus saith the LORD, Make this valley full of ditches. For . . . Ye shall not see wind, neither shall ye see rain; yet that valley shall be filled with water,*

that ye may drink, both ye, and your
cattle, and your beasts. And this is but
a light thing in the sight of the LORD:
he will deliver the Moabites also into
your hand (II Kings 3:16-18).

I'm sure at this point Jehoram was not feeling well at all. First, he thought that God was mad at him and death was just around the corner. Then he heard the word of the Lord through Elisha telling them that they had to dig ditches! And worst of all, the ditches had to be dug in the middle of a hot, dusty valley.

Have you ever noticed that God doesn't always perform an earth-shattering event when miracles are needed? God is very practical. He wants to use us to accomplish the desired goal. If we have to dig ditches to gain the victory, then we better do as God says and dig ditches!

Sometimes Christians feel "too spiritual" to work hard at the practical things God wants accomplished. Serving coffee at a church function may not seem glorious or even inspiring. But God is simply wild over the fact that you would give of your time and effort to an important cause. The simple act of serving others may be just the key *you* need to bring about *your* miracle.

The men began to dig the ditches just as God had said. Dig, dig, dig. First one ditch, then another ditch, and another, and soon it was ditches here, there, and everywhere.

Finally, the ditch digging was over. Then the men put their tools away and waited. And they waited some more. But nothing happened. All that hot and tiring work, and still the water had not appeared.

THE CHALLENGE OF A MIRACLE

Miracles don't always happen instantly. Sometimes you have really believed God for a particular situation, and you've claimed that miracle; but no matter how hard you continue to pray—nothing seems to happen. Days, weeks, even months can go by with no outward sign that God is even interested in your problem.

The devil loves to come during these times and tell us that God has no intention of helping us. "See," the devil says, "I told you all that prayer and fasting for a miracle was no good! God doesn't care about your problems. You're not going to get a miracle so why don't you just give up and forget it!"

With the devil's lies comes fear, and fear robs us of our faith. Without faith in God our hope is lost; and suddenly we don't trust God to bring our miracles into existence. At that moment the devil has us precisely where he wants us!

The men were exhausted. They had spent hours in a dry, hot valley digging ditches for reasons they didn't even understand. And now, after hours of waiting, the ditches were still as dry as a bone, and there was no sign of water.

Talk about discouragement! The armies of Jehoram, Jehoshaphat, and Edom probably wanted to pack up and move out. They had had enough of this foolishness for one day, and there was no use sticking around. Nothing was going to happen anyway—so they thought.

But here is the challenge of a miracle. Some miracles take time. And if we don't purpose in our hearts to stay with God, then we will miss the miracle. God's timing is different than our timing, and patience is the key needed to win. With faith and patience working for us, we will see the miracle come at just the perfect time.

When I was about 20 years old, my mother went on an extended fast for 21 days. When I asked her why she was fasting, she said it was for me! I was so disappointed when I heard that because surely everyone knew that I didn't need prayer and fasting! Well, my mother also said she was fasting for my brother and father because they needed the Lord.

At the end of 21 days, my mother ended her fast. My father still wasn't serving God, my brother wasn't saved, and I hadn't been baptized with the

Holy Spirit. At this point my mother could have said, "Okay God, I guess the miracles I was believing for are never coming to pass; so I'll just stop praying about them." But that wasn't what my mother let her heart believe. She held on to the Word and continued to pray for her miracles. The end result was that both my father and my brother became born again. And obviously God got a hold of my life; because I am in full-time ministry.

Next time the devil challenges you about receiving your miracle, remember to challenge him with the Word of God. That should take care of his accusations and fill you with even more faith to believe for your miracle.

LAST-MINUTE MIRACLES

Just at the moment when you think the miracle will never appear, God intervenes:

And it came to pass in the morning, when the meat offering was offered, that, behold, there came water by the way of Edom and the country was filled with water (II Kings 3:20).

The miracle didn't occur at the time the ditches were dug. The miracle appeared at the time of the morning sacrifice, when praise and worship were being offered unto the Lord. That may not have been their timing for the miracle of water to appear, but it was the exact instant that God wanted it to appear.

God is not slothful about time. He is the best organizer of time I know! He sees ahead into the future and knows just when a miracle is going to be needed. In Jesus, all of our miracles are there just for the asking. They have our names on them, and He is just waiting for us to claim them!

When we pray for miracles, we need to be specific. We need to tell God our concerns and needs, but we don't need to pray with an attitude of fear—thinking that God will be late with the miracle. Mark 11:24 says:

" . . . *What things soever ye desire,*
when ye pray, believe that ye receive
them, and ye shall have them.''

The Bible doesn't say, "What things soever you desire, when you pray, believe that you receive them, unless the kids are sick, your finances are low, and the miracles are late." God is *not* a procrastinator; He is never, ever late to bring the supernatural into our lives when we believe for it.

THE EXAMPLE
OF THE MIRACLE

Miracles are an example of God's grace. God will go around a thousand obstacles to bring the supernatural to us because of Jesus Christ. And not only does the miracle cause us to triumph over the circumstances, it also teaches us more about God and gives us examples of godly living.

You recall that in the early morning hours God had caused the ditches to fill with water. I'm sure the armies of men and the kings were ecstatic over this finding. But what about the Moabites? Didn't Jehoram, Jehoshaphat, and the king of Edom still have a battle on their hands?

> . . . *when all the Moabites heard that the kings were come up to fight against them, they gathered all that were able to put on armour, and upward, and stood in the border. And they rose up early in the morning, and the sun shone upon the water, and the Moabites saw the water on the other side as red as blood: And they said, This is blood: the kings are surely slain, and they have smitten one another: now therefore, Moab, to the spoil* (II Kings 3:21-23).

The men of Moab had heard about Jehoram, Jehoshaphat, and the king of Edom coming to fight. They had prepared themselves by gathering up all the able young men of the city and enrolling them in Basic Army 101. The men of Moab had no intention of losing this one.

As the dawn's early light shown down on the

water-filled ditches, the men of Moab could not believe their eyes! Instead of seeing water, Moab thought they were seeing blood! The glow of the morning sun made the water look red like blood, and Moab was convinced the armies of Judah, Israel, and Edom had killed each other. "Off to the spoil!" cried Moab, as they headed into the valley to take the dead men's belongings.

Sometimes we as Christians rush out ahead of God. We think we have seen the green light, and we plunge straight ahead without God's permission. Later, we usually find ourselves knee-deep in trouble and wonder where in the world God could be! It always pays to wait upon God and to listen to His voice first.

The Moabites were having a great day so far. The kings and armies of their attackers had turned on each other and killed one another—so they thought. It was a big bloodbath down in the valley, and the Moabites were going to loot and steal from the belongings of the dead men. What a perfect outing for that day!

But God had another idea in mind for the Moabites:

> . . . when they came to the camp of Israel, the Israelites rose up and smote the Moabites, so that they fled before them: but they went forward smiting the Moabites, even in their country (II Kings 3:24).

The Moabites soon discovered that the valley was not full of dead bodies, but of living, breathing, fighting men! The camp of the Israelites was so strong that they chased the men of Moab back into their own country. Then the Israelites plundered the city, cut off all the wells, and even chopped down all the good trees! Moab was utterly defeated at the hands of Jehoshaphat's army.

God had granted Jehoshaphat a tremendous miracle! His men were overwhelmingly victorious over Moab. The miracle was a great example not only to Jehoshaphat but also to Jehoram and the king of Edom. God had kept His promise and had proved, once again, His faithfulness to bless the righteous.

Miracles happen today just like they did in Jehoshaphat's time. They had a wonderful sign of God's grace and mercy, and God loves to give us hope to help in our time of need.

Now put your hand over your heart and say this with me:

M = The MAKING of a Miracle
I = The IMMEDIACY of a Miracle
R = The RECEIVING of a Miracle
A = The ACCOMPLISHING of a Miracle
C = The CHALLENGE of a Miracle
L = The LAST MINUTE of a Miracle
E = The EXAMPLE of a Miracle

Put these seed words of faith into your heart and begin to believe God for your miracle today!

Chapter Two

MIRACLES IN YOU

Everybody needs a miracle at one time or another in their lives. Problems hit people no matter where they live or what they do. If you are rich and handsome, you will still have problems. If you are a hermit living alone on a deserted island, I have news for you; you will still have problems. Problems are not respecters of education, bank accounts, race, sex, or even good intentions. Every person alive on this earth has been hit with trials and hardships. The devil would love for these trials to whittle us slowly but surely down to nothing and cause our lives to be completely hopeless.

If I stopped here, you might think, "Marilyn, I'm depressed! You mean I'm always going to have problems? Is the devil going to keep me down and out of it all of my life?" Well, I have good news for you: Jesus Christ came to destroy the works of the devil. We don't have to live a defeated life on this earth. Jesus doesn't cut us down with problems. He builds us up with supercharged miracles! Christians are born of incorruptible seed and have the blueprint for success inside them. For every problem the devil throws at us, we have a miracle waiting. And that miracle is in your faith in Jesus Christ.

PREPARING
FOR A MIRACLE

When we are getting ready to plant a garden, we know that we first must prepare the ground. If the soil is full of rocks, we need to get a wheelbarrow and haul away the rocks. If the soil is sandy, then we need to buy lots of topsoil in order to give the ground the proper nutrients. Rocky and sandy soil will not produce a healthy garden because the ground is not fertile enough to sustain plant growth.

Do you know that Christians sometimes have a hard time producing a bountiful harvest in their lives because their hearts are full of rocks and sand? If we haven't taken the time to prepare our hearts with the Word of God and prayer, then miracles will have a hard time growing. God gives us the seed for a miracle before we even need it. But if our hearts are cold and hard, then the seed of faith will eventually die.

I remember a letter I received from a woman in San Antonio whose husband was going through a very difficult time. The man had been put in jail for molesting a child. Even though he was innocent, he just happened to look like the man who had actually committed the crime.

Now the husband and wife were not Christians when all this mess started. However, during this stressful time, someone shared the Lord with them; and they both became born again. They began to put their faith in God and trust Him for a miracle to turn around the situation.

One day I was doing my radio broadcast, and the wife was listening. I gave a scripture from the book of Esther and then said, ''In 24 days you are going to have a miracle.'' The woman was in such despair and needed a miracle badly. She quickly counted the number of days until her husband's trial. It just so happened to be 24 days away!

I used to tape my radio broadcasts at least two months ahead. Of course, it's impossible for me to know the future needs of people, but the Holy Spirit knows, right? The Holy Spirit had given that scripture and word of knowledge to this woman to comfort her and assure her of a miracle. Now if that woman had had a hard and rebellious heart, she might not have received the word from the Lord. She could have said, "Oh brother! This is never going to work! My husband will be found guilty, and he'll be thrown in jail for 20 years! This is horrible, horrible, horrible!"

But hearts that have been prepared with the Word and with prayer are good soil in which miracles can grow. That woman received the promise of a miracle into her heart and when her husband's trial date arrived, he was found completely innocent! The woman had prepared her heart to receive a miracle. And when the time came, the miracle came forth! (Interestingly enough, her name was Esther!)

PLANTING
A MIRACLE

In II Kings 2 we see an unusual situation that doesn't look very hopeful. When it seemed that things were going from bad to worse, the men of Jericho called upon Elisha, the prophet of God, to help them:

And the men of the city said unto Elisha, Behold, I pray thee, the situation of this city is pleasant, as my lord seeth: but the water is naught, and the ground barren (II Kings 2:19).

Elisha had a very big problem on his hands. It appeared that the water of the city was not very good. The Hebrew translation says that water was "evil" or "exceedingly harmful." The prophets had explained to Elisha that all the other parts of the city were nice and lovely, but this water problem was causing some real aches and pains. The water would come forth and water the trees, yet the fruit of the trees would never come to full maturity. The cattle would take of the water, but often they would miscarry their young. It was really a terrible situation.

Let's look at the background of the situation for a moment. Jericho was a cursed city. No, God didn't just wake up one day and decide to curse a city, and then proclaim that Jericho was the place. In Leviticus, God said that if a city was involved in idolatry and sacrificing its children to idols, that city was a cursed place and should be wiped out. God also said that any city that was involved in sexual sin was a cursed place. Well, Jericho was involved with both idol worship and sexual sin. Therefore, Jericho was cursed because of its sin, and the water was one of the evidences of the curse.

The people of Jericho had a big problem. They lived in a cursed city, and they didn't know what to do. The water was bitter and awful to drink, the plants wouldn't grow, and the animals had trouble bearing offspring. This sounds like a soap opera, doesn't it? But Jericho, the cursed city, is just the kind of place where God would love to do a miracle. God hates the sin, but He's wild over the people.

Now Elisha was a man of God in every way. His heart was not full of rocks and sand. He had fed on the Word of God, and had given himself to much prayer. Elisha was prepared to get a miracle because his heart was made out of good soil. But Elisha knew that he was going to have to do something in order to get that miracle. He was going to have to activate that seed of faith and to plant it so that it would grow into the miracle he needed.

We all know that once we have prepared the ground for the garden, the next step is actually to plant the seeds. You know, as long as those seeds are in their packet, they won't do anything. You can ask them to grow, but nothing will happen. You can even get a little mean and yell at them to grow, but again, nothing will happen. Why? Because you have to plant the seeds in that wonderfully fertile soil you have prepared. Seeds need nutrients from the soil, water, and sunshine to grow. Without these essentials, the seeds either will remain dormant or simply die.

I know some people that are dormant Christians. You may think, "Marilyn, that's a terrible thing to say!" But it's true! When problems come, they yell and scream and pout at the situation; but they don't use the Word of God to help them. Yelling and even stomping your feet at a problem may help you feel better for a moment. But all that exercise doesn't put a dent in the situation itself. Only faith mixed with God's Word will change the circumstances.

WATERING
THE MIRACLE

Elisha had prepared his heart for the miracle. He had planted the seed of faith and was seeking God about what he should do next. You see, Elisha was being positive about the whole thing. He didn't say, "This is an impossible job! You can't change something that has been cursed! Besides, I don't know anything about fixing bitter water! Go ask someone else." Elisha knew that his God was a God of miracles, and Elisha was going to hang on until he got his miracle.

Sometimes when we get into tough circumstances, we've prepared our hearts enough to withstand the first attack of the devil. We've planted our faith in the Word of God, and we just know that if we stand firm, our miracle will come. Everything seems to go well for awhile, but then the devil shows up again.

The devil lies and says that the miracle is never coming. Your faith begins to weaken because of discouragement and despair. The devil talks again and more discouragement and unbelief are produced. Soon, there is no faith or hope left that the miracle will ever come.

What happened? When you planted your garden, you first prepared the ground. Next, you planted the seeds in the dirt. Then you turned to your spouse and said, "There honey! I'll never, ever have to care for this garden again! I'm all finished!"

Fourteen days later, after several days of 90 degree weather, you go out to check on this marvelous garden. You're just sure that the lettuce is up and ready to eat. But, to your surprise, you don't see much of anything. Most of the seeds never germinated and sprouted. Those that did germinate stand very small and withered. It appears that the only minor detail you forgot was the water!

Just as there are several steps in planting a garden, there are also several steps in getting your miracle. Some Christians give up in the preparation stage because their hearts are hard and rocky. Some people give up after the planting stage— because results don't come in fast enough to please them.

Instead, Christians should get out their Bibles and water themselves with the Word so that their faith stays strong. There's an old saying: "The race isn't always to the swiftest, but to those who keep on running." God doesn't want us to stop believing for our miracles. Rather, He wants us to tie a knot on the end of the rope and hang on until the miracle manifests.

FEEDING
A MIRACLE

The city of Jericho needed a miracle in the worst way. Somehow that curse had to be turned into a blessing, and the men of the city were trusting Elisha to do the job.

Have you noticed whom the men of the city chose to help them in their time of need? They certainly didn't go and ask one of their idols for help. The men chose Elisha because of his faith in God's miracle-growing ability! *Elisha* means, "Jehovah is salvation," and Jericho needed to be saved and delivered from their curse.

Despite all the confusion circling through the city about how to fix the water and how to erase the curse from Jericho's past, Elisha remained perfectly calm. He was positive in his heart about what God could do, and he prepared his heart to receive a miracle:

> ". . . *Bring me a new cruse, and put salt therein. And they brought it to him*" (II Kings 2:20).

As you can see, Elisha did not stand over the waters with his hands spread wide yelling, "Thou foul and evil water, I rebuke thee! Be pleasant tasting and nutritious from this day forward!" Elisha was practical and he asked for something simple. He wanted a jar or bowl that had never

31

been used, and he wanted the new bowl to have some salt inside. No fancy preaching—no fancy equipment. The people may have been puzzled by Elisha's unusual request!

Yes, the people could very well have reasoned away what God had told them to do through Elisha. They could have murmured, "We have rotten water, sick plants, and dying baby animals; and this guy wants us to get him a new bowl with salt in it. Ugh! Now, instead of plain bitter water, we can have bitter, salty water!" Jericho could have written off Elisha as a sick, sick man and looked for someone else to help. But, fortunately, the people obeyed Elisha and were able to be a part of a miracle in progress.

As Christians we have to be careful that we don't give up on the miracle before it comes. We can prepare, plant, and water our miracle seed faithfully every day. Yet sometimes we still have to go one step further.

When our little garden plants first start to grow, they look green and healthy. Just as hot sun, dry soil, bugs, and wind can take their toil on little garden plants, a similar thing can happen to Christians. Every once and awhile we need an extra boost, so that we don't give up on our miracles. That extra boost comes from the Word of God.

The Bible is called the Bread of Life because

it gives life to our spiritual self. Reading the promises of God feeds us and causes our faith to grow into a full maturity. When our miracle hasn't come and hasn't come and hasn't come, that's when God's Word can refresh us and revitalize us for the duration of the battle.

Elisha knew the miracle for the bitter water was coming forth. He had prepared his heart and planted the seed of faith. He had watered the miracle with the Word, and now Elisha was going to feed others the Word of truth by example.

HARVESTING A MIRACLE

Have you ever noticed that most construction projects begin with a blueprint? Blueprints are the instructions for the design and layout of the building. If the person creating the blueprint has made a mistake somewhere, the building will probably be built with that mistake in it. Blueprints are essential and must be followed carefully so that the building is erected successfully.

When God created man, He created him from three different blueprints: a spiritual blueprint, an intellectual/emotional blueprint, and a body blueprint. Perhaps the blueprint for the body read something like, "Connect the hip bone to the leg bone, not the hip bone to the neck bone." Perhaps the blueprint for the intellect or mind said, "This symbol is equal to a letter, and a series of letters is equal to a word and many words together make a sentence and this is how you read." You can see already how important it is for the blueprint to be correct so that the parts can fit together.

God also has given us a marvelous spiritual blueprint. Inside each print are the seeds for success. Some of those seeds are faith seeds, hope seeds, and patience seeds. Still others are miracle seeds.

When a farmer goes out to plant his field, he begins with the later intention of harvesting a good crop. He wants to make sure that all his work ends up with a successful harvest. Likewise, when Jesus went to the Cross, He already had looked into the future. He knew that the Cross was only temporary, but the harvest of souls was eternal. Jesus willingly gave up His own life because by His death a harvest of millions would be saved.

We know that inside our blueprints are the seeds for success. But do you know that Christians are born of a seed? You may say, "Oh brother! Now I have heard everything!" But it's true! First Peter 1:23 says:

> *"Being born again, not of corruptible seed, but of incorruptible, by the word of God, which liveth and abideth forever."*

Something that is corruptible means that it is perishable. But incorruptible means that it will not perish or fade away. It will live on and on into eternity.

When you were born again, you received the imperishable Word of life into your heart. The Word of God became the incorruptible seed that sealed your salvation. The Bible says that everything else will pass away, but the Word of God will last forever. That Word of God became the incorruptible seed of life in you.

Jesus came to give that imperishable seed to all that would believe. He became the Word in flesh form. When He died on the Cross, He planted His life as a seed, and from Him came a harvest of millions. Jesus was the firstborn of many, and all who receive the seed of life become new creations in Christ:

> *Therefore if any man be in Christ, he is a new creature: old things are passed away; behold, all things are become new* (II Corinthians 5:17).

New creations in Christ are full of the life of God. All the old junk and trash of the past is dead and buried. When the imperishable seed of the Word of God begins to grow and change you into the likeness of Jesus, people will notice. They will say, "Hey, isn't that so-and-so who used to be such a pain? I wonder what happened to him? He's so nice!'' Jesus took away all those old, yucky habits and gave you good, godly habits!

One of the reasons people notice a change in you is because you are salty. You may not believe me, but the Bible says that you are the salt of the earth. Do you know that salt is very important to God? Salt was used in every one of the major offerings of the Old Testament covenants. It was used as a form of agreement between the people and God. When you accept Jesus, you become salty because you become a covenant partner with God. He sees you as the salt of the world.

Why did God choose to call us salt? When you study salt, you will see that it has many interesting qualities. It is a preservative that keeps things from spoiling; it prevents corruption; and, many years ago, salt was given to guests as an expression of hospitality.

If salt is a preserver, then we Christians need to take our salt into the world and snatch precious lives from the hands of the devil. Passing our salt along will help preserve others and deliver them from the corruption of the world.

Remember Elisha and the new jar filled with salt? Well, Christians are a lot like new jars filled with salt. We are new creations filled with miracle-working power. When people see miracles flowing from our lives, they get curious. Our salt rubs off on them, and they get thirsty. Soon, they want to know all about Jesus.

Elisha knew that the new jar with salt in it would be the tool for the miracle. He had done the preparation, planting, watering, and fertilizing. Now it was time to harvest the miracle:

> *And he went forth unto the spring of the waters, and cast the salt in there, and said, Thus saith the LORD, I have healed these waters; there shall not be from thence any more death or barren land. So the waters were healed unto this day, . . .* (II Kings 2:21,22).

Elisha didn't take the jar with salt and put it 100 feet from the water. The problem was the water, so he put the salt directly in the water. The instant the salt hit the water a miracle took place; the water was healed. The harvest of healing had taken place.

Christians have the seeds of miracles inside them because they have Jesus inside them. With Jesus you have the miracle of healing. Healed bodies, healed pocketbooks, and healed minds are good examples. Just as the new jar with salt healed the water, Christians heal the surrounding situation because Jesus, the miracle-giver, lives inside them.

A few years ago I went camping with some dear friends. Now, I'm not a real fan of camping, but I decided to go anyway. Just before we left, my mother had gone through a routine medical checkup. But the news was bad: my mother had a brain tumor.

As I lay in that little trailer looking up at the stars, I began to worry about my mother. But then I remembered that Jesus lived in me, and He designed me for success. I knew that I had those miracle seeds inside me.

I began to pray and ask God for a miracle. I quoted Psalm 107:20:

> *"He sent his word, and healed them, and delivered them from their destructions."*

I pictured my mother's head in my mind, and I focused on that brain tumor. I prayed, "Father, I send the Word into that brain tumor. Your Word goes into that brain tumor, heals her brain, and delivers her from the destruction of that tumor." I prepared for a miracle, and I wasn't going to give up until I saw the harvest of that miracle. When my mother went back to the doctor to check on the tumor, they x-rayed her head. And guess what? There was not even one sign that a tumor had been present. I had used the Word of God to send my mother a miracle. God's Word never, ever fails.

MIRACLES
IN YOU

When you visit Jericho today, you will see beautiful palm trees and fruit trees. Harvest season is a wonderful time because everything grows so well. The cattle don't miscarry their young, and the water is some of the sweetest water you have ever tasted.

Jericho turned from being a cursed place to a blessed place. The people of the city wanted a miracle to turn their situation around. They found a godly man who knew that the seed of a miracle was inside him. A new jar filled with salt symbolically lifted Jericho from death into new life.

You don't have to keep living in bad situations. You don't have to allow the devil to ruin your life. If Jesus lives in you, so do miracles. Your spirit man has been born of incorruptible seed, and the life force of God resides in you. When Jesus comes into your heart, the old passes away and everything is becoming new. No longer do seeds of fear and doubt control the garden of your mind and heart; instead, seeds of faith and miracles are growing. Soon you will harvest miracles instead of trouble and despair.

God loves people who stick with a job and don't give up. Stick-to-it Christians prepare for a miracle and don't give up until they harvest their miracle. Rain, hail, and worms can come and try to kill their miracle, but they just fight harder. They want their miracle more than anything else.

Miracles are in you because Jesus Christ is in you. You must be a new jar filled with the salt of God's Word. There can be miracles everyplace you go. Curses can be changed into blessings. Families can be changed. Governments can be changed. Broken hearts can be healed. I don't care how bad the situation looks, a miracle can turn it around. Why? Because faith inside you provides the potential for every miracle you will ever need!

Chapter Three
MOVING
IN
THE
MIRACULOUS

Reading about miracles is always very encouraging. When God turns *devastating* situations into *divine situations*, we feel encouraged in our hearts. Why? Because we know that He can do the same for us. God does not prefer one person over another. He doesn't say, "I'm sorry, but I can't give you a miracle because your hair is too straight." God isn't a mean old man sitting in heaven waiting to hit you with a baseball bat. He loves you! God is the greatest giver in the world, and He loves to give miracles to His children.

We know miracles happened during Old and New Testament history. Men and women of God prayed and received miracles left and right. Some of the prophets of the Old Testament probably didn't even blink an eye when they got miracles because they were so used to them! As the people grew in the Lord, they not only received miracles to get out of a crisis, but they began to give miracles to other people in crises! When the people of God started moving in the miraculous, the course of human history changed. We all know that in the New Testament Jesus began walking in the miraculous after He was baptized with the Holy Spirit. Soon His disciples got so used to seeing miracles, they trusted the power of God and began ministering in miracles too. The things of God are contagious because God is such a good

God. When we see Him giving us miracles, then we begin to minister miracles to others. Because we have received of His goodness and mercy, we want to give goodness and mercy.

Some Christians may feel very confident about asking God to give them a miracle. They may go through some really tough times, but they hang in there. They want that miracle and they won't give up. These Christians are what we call *tenacious*. *Tenacious* means, "not easily pulled apart; tending to cling or adhere; sticky." Christians who won't let go of their miracle are sticky: they are sticking to God and sticking to the Word; they won't let the devil defeat them. God loves sticky Christians!

LAYING A FOUNDATION FOR MIRACLES

When we build something, it is imperative that we lay a good foundation. Without a good foundation, the structure will eventually collapse. Do you remember seeing that apartment building that collapsed in on itself during the California earthquake? When the earthquake hit, the pressure and tension of the moving earth on the foundation proved to be too much. The foundation no doubt gave way, allowing the building to collapse. That is why a foundation is so important—it remains strong and sure when the world gets shaky.

When we are growing in the Lord, we must build a good foundation for ourselves. A good foundation includes time for prayer and reading the Word; belonging to a good church is also important. If we build our lives with a little prayer here, and a little church there, what we have is a shaky foundation. And when that old troublemaker the devil comes at us, we will crumble because we have not built ourselves up in the Lord.

In order to minister miracles to others, we must make sure that our own foundations are strong. Weak foundations produce little, tiny miracles. Strong foundations produce great, big miracles. And I know that great, big miracles are needed much more frequently than the little ones.

But how do we check our foundations? We can get out a flashlight and check the structural foundation of our homes. But we can't use a flashlight on ourselves. One way to check is to look at some Biblical examples of people who walked in the miraculous.

THE EXAMPLE OF OTHERS

The Bible says not to be associated with

people who walk in darkness. That must mean that God wants us to walk with people who walk in the light. Good examples benefit us because they help us grow stronger. Jesus was the best example of ''light'' that the world has ever had. His light continues to shine forth through people like you and me. Being with other Christians charges our batteries and makes us shine brighter. And following the example of other bright-light Christians helps our lights shine even more brilliantly.

In preceding chapters we've spent quite a bit of time in the book of II Kings studying about kings and prophets of God who received some outstanding miracles in their lives. Two of the most well-known prophets are Elijah and Elisha. Elijah was the first prophet and Elisha was the second one. You can remember them alphabetically. ''J'' comes before ''S'' so Elijah is the first one.

The Bible has something very interesting to say about doing things in pairs. Elijah moved in the miraculous but his ministry was incomplete without Elisha. John 8:17 says:

"It is also written in your law, that the testimony of two men is true."

So one person brings forth one part of the testimony and the other person brings forth the second part of the testimony. When you put the two together, you have a complete picture.

In the Old Testament we have witnesses whose lives are contrasted and witnesses whose lives agree. Let's look at some contrasts first. When I give you the name Cain, who do you think of next? If you thought of Abel, you're right. Cain and Abel were the first set of brothers on the earth. You would have thought that since they were the first brothers that they would have been good examples. But Cain was the bad guy and Abel was the good guy, and so we have a contrast. Cain said he could "do his own thing" and Abel said, "No way!" And we know the results were not good between these brothers: in a fit of jealousy, Cain killed his brother.

Then we have Abraham and Lot. Abraham was the father of faith, but Lot was the father of sense knowledge. Lot did not make good faith choices or walk by the Word. Abraham and Lot were good examples: one walked by the Word of God and was successful, while the other walked by his senses and was unsuccessful.

Isaac and Ishmael, the sons of Abraham, were half-brothers. Isaac, born of Sarah, was the child of promise; while Ishmael, born of Hagar, was a child born of the flesh. One walked by the Spirit and one by the flesh. The Bible says in Galatians that we are not to walk after the flesh but after the Spirit because the Spirit always brings life into our situations.

Enoch was the man who prophesied that there would be a flood, and Noah was the man who was a part of the flood. If we only had Enoch's story, we wouldn't have a complete picture. If we only read about Noah and the flood and didn't know the events that preceded it, then, again the picture would be incomplete. The two witnesses help us join parts of the Bible together so we can understand God's plan better.

Remember Moses and Aaron? Moses was called by God to lead the Israelites out of slavery, but he was a crybaby at first. He told God he couldn't talk very well; and, therefore, he really wouldn't be the best man for the job. God said, "Okay, Aaron will do the talking." So Aaron became the spokesman, and his rod was used over and over again to perform miracles. It was Aaron's rod that Moses used to bring on the plagues. Moses wasn't complete without Aaron, and Aaron wasn't complete without Moses.

Now let's look at John the Baptist and Jesus. John the Baptist was not a sissy; he told it like it was and called people to repent and turn to God. He even called the people snakes, which was really turning on the steam. John was preparing the way for Jesus.

Then along came Jesus, and He walked through the open door that had been prepared by

John. People had been told to repent and turn to God; and, at just the proper time Jesus came and showed the way. Without John, people would not have been ready for Jesus. Jesus was the completion of John's prophecy.

Jesus said that when He was on the earth He performed miracles as God worked through Him. When Jesus returned to heaven, He sent us the Holy Spirit. By sending the Holy Spirit to work through us, Jesus could continue seeing miracles happen on the earth. Without Jesus *we* could not do miracles. Together we have a complete picture.

With that as a background, we can understand the ministries of Elijah and Elisha a little better. Elijah was a very powerful and mighty prophet; and, therefore, God used him in miracles of judgment. He prayed and commanded the heavens to be closed and the heavens were closed. He prayed and commanded the heavens to be opened, and they were opened. Then he prayed fire down; and, sure enough, down came the fire. Elijah's miracles were centered around the judgment of the people for their sin.

Then came Elisha, and his miracles were entirely different. Elisha did not have a judgment motive but a mercy motive. His miracles were much, much different because he was representing the merciful side of God. We know that God is not only a God of judgment but a God of mercy too.

Elijah and Elisha are two parts of a picture that came together to make a whole. Elisha saw that Elijah moved in the miraculous, and Elisha wanted to do the same. Elisha watched Elijah carefully because he was setting a good example. We'll see at the end that Elisha got the double portion from Elijah and also began to move in the miraculous.

It's good for us to study other people and see how they built their foundations. Cain didn't do such a hot job with his, but Abel received eternal life. Lot's life was so full of death, but Abraham's was full of life. Moses didn't want to talk, so Aaron became his spokesman. Elijah called down fire but Elisha poured on the mercy. Some people had good foundations and their lives were full of the miraculous. When we compare our lives to the lives of people who were successful and full of miracles, then we are inspired to complete the picture by fixing our foundations so we, too, can walk in the miraculous.

LAYING HOLD OF THE MIRACULOUS

I believe all Christians should expect to see the miraculous in their lives. Too many times I think we accept defeat because we don't really expect the supernatural to work in our circumstances. You know, athletes spend thousands of hours training to win. They didn't start their vigorous training programs with the intent to fail. If gold-medal winners started out training to lose, and that was their goal, they would never achieve that prestigious medal.

Like athletes, Christians are in training too. We train to pray an hour, train to apply the Word to our lives, and train to walk in the Spirit. Living a godly life takes practice, practice, and even more practice. When times of discouragement and despair come knocking at our doors, our first reactions will be based on the hours of practice. If our training was haphazard, so will be our miracles. But if we diligently applied ourselves to God's training plan, then we should be strong and able to defeat the devil. God made us to win, and miracles are the "gold medals" of our victories.

ACTING LIKE A WINNER

In our story about Elijah and Elisha, we know that Elijah was a winner. Elijah knew how to get ahold of the miraculous, and when Elijah talked, people listened! Elisha was so impressed with

Elijah that he wanted to be just like him. If Elijah could be a winner, Elisha knew he could be the same. So Elisha began to "train" to be like Elijah. He probably said, "Whatever Elijah does, I'm going to do the same. Whatever Elijah says, I'm going to say. Whatever Elijah eats, I'm going to eat! I want to walk in miracles just like Elijah, so I'll be a copycat!"

Well, what do you suppose happened to Elisha? After Elijah was caught away in the whirlwind, Elisha began to get ahold of miracles. He practiced what he had heard Elijah say when the prophet began to prepare for a miracle:

> . . . *As the LORD God of Israel liveth, before whom I stand, there shall not be dew nor rain these years, but according to my word* (I Kings 17:1).

And no rain fell for three years. Later Elisha copied Elijah and said:

> " . . . *As the LORD of hosts liveth, before whom I stand . . .* "
> (II Kings 3:14).

—and then a miracle unfolded. By copying a winner, Elisha became a winner too.

Copying or imitating other successful Christians is alright because it helps us recharge our batteries and give off more light to the world. But what God really wants us to do is to copy

Jesus—because if there ever was a winner, it was Jesus.

Jesus didn't come to the earth and decide to do things His own way. Jesus knew that if He wanted to be successful, then He had to copy His Father. John 5:19 says:

> ... *The Son can do nothing of*
> *himself, but what he seeth the Father*
> *do: for what things soever he doeth,*
> *these also doeth the Son likewise.*

Jesus copied His Father and walked in the miraculous. He didn't bow His knees to defeat everytime He saw someone oppressed of the devil. Jesus acted like the winner God made Him to be, and miracles were a part of His everyday life.

If we want miracles to be a part of our everyday lives, then we must act like Jesus in everything we do. Imitating Jesus is part of God's training program. God says, ''If you want to be successful and reap miracles in your life, then copy My Son Jesus.'' One way of copying Jesus is to talk like Him. Jesus said that the words that He spoke were the same words His Father spoke.

When a situation looks bad, we shouldn't say, ''This is really going to ruin me; I'm going to fail and lose everything; I'll never be a success.'' If you speak these words and believe them in your heart, then you are not copying the words of Jesus. Jesus· doesn't speak of gloom and doom and failure. But I'll tell you who does speak of defeat and despair—the devil! Those are the only words he knows because his whole life has been a failure. If the devil can get you to put your faith in what he says, then he can rob you of your winning attitude and your miracle.

Once Wally and I got on a plane in Dallas that was headed for Mexico. As I was sitting in back, a man approached me and said he had seen me on some of Bob Tilton's satellite programs. He then proceeded to tell me that he had only been a Christian six months, but he had really backslidden and gotten back into drinking. He was also going to Mexico, and he was really afraid that he was going to slip even further and get into adultery and other kinds of junk and trash.

Well, this man just kept confessing all the devil's lies to me; and finally, I said "You are not going to get drunk, and you're not going to get into adultery. I don't care if the devil is after you; the Bible says that He Who is in you is greater than he that is in the world." Then I told him that sin couldn't have dominion over him because Jesus was in him. The man said he just didn't think he could overcome these temptations. I told him to be quiet and to put his hand on his heart and say, "I can do all things through Christ Who strengthens me."

I had one of those little "Speak the Word"

booklets with me, and I gave one to him. I said to him, "Quit speaking what the devil tells you, and start speaking what God says about you. Every morning when you get up, I want you to get on your knees and pray for 20 minutes and then read your Bible for 20 minutes. Then you can go out in the strength of the Lord."

This man probably thought he had just received shock treatment after I was through speaking to him. But let me tell you what happened. As we were waiting at the Mexico airport to go back to Denver, who do you think we saw but that *same man!* He came running over with his face beaming and his heart full of joy. He said, "I've got to tell you what happened! I did just what you said. I got up every morning and prayed and read my Bible. I read scriptures to the man I was staying with and I wouldn't drink with him. He couldn't figure out why I was on my knees praying and reading the Bible; but, after five or six days, the man got so curious that I led him to Christ!"

RENEWING YOUR MIND

Do you understand what really happened to the man I met on the plane? He started to speak what Jesus said instead of what the devil said. He stopped listening to doom and gloom and got turned on to the Word. The more he spoke Jesus' words, the more his mind became renewed to the truth. The Bible says that the truth sets you free; and, the man was set free from junk and trash and got a miracle.

If your parents and friends always told you that you were fat, ugly, and no good, you might have started to believe them because your mind believed the lies. Then the devil probably told you that you would never be a success at relationships or business ventures or personal endeavors because you were such a failure anyway. So you go along feeling like a used rag until someone turns you on to Jesus and you get born again. Suddenly you realize that you have been bought with a price and are worth something in this world. Instead of believing lies and speaking doubt and unbelief, you start to act like Jesus and speak His words. You begin to act like a winner; and, for the first time, there is success in your life.

However, twenty days after you are born again your car breaks down, the bathroom sink plugs up, and the perm in your hair falls out. You feel like a wreck and look like one too. And all those words of despair and discouragement rise up out of you like a flood. You want to believe God for a miracle, but the devil's lies keep you down and out. The problem here is that your mind hasn't been renewed to the Word of Truth, which can set you free.

Sometimes we come to the Lord with a lot of old habit patterns that don't leave right away. We have to keep the "training" program going to renew our minds. By speaking the words of Jesus and imitating Him in action, soon we will see those old mental patterns disappear once and for all. Now when trials come against us, we can speak the Word of life into the situation and grab onto the miraculous.

MINISTERING IN THE MIRACULOUS

So far we've learned a lot about building strong foundations by copying the godly examples of others, speaking the words of Jesus, and renewing our minds to the Word. We've learned that building an unshakable foundation requires lots of "training" and preparation for success. If you want to be a winner, then you have to act like a winner. When we build our foundations on Jesus and act like winners, then we open the door for miracles.

Remember when we talked about "tenacious" or "sticky" Christians? Those are the kinds of Christians God loves because they tend to cling or "stick" to the Word. When the time comes for a miracle, sticky Christians speak the words of Jesus, renew their minds with the Word, copy the examples of other godly people, and act like winners.

But sometimes these same sticky Christians don't think they can minister miracles to others. "Oh, dear, I could never lay my hands on this sister and believe for a healing miracle! I'm just not good enough! This is a job for Dr. Cho or Kenneth Copeland!" But we know the Word tells us differently. When Jesus left the earth, He gave us the Holy Spirit so we could walk in power and might. He also left us with some instructions, and they don't say, "Pray for a miracle for sister so and so—but only on Tuesdays and Thursdays, at the stroke of midnight, will you get a 50/50 chance of getting that miracle." The Bible clearly instructs us to minister to the sick, the poor, the broken-hearted, and all those oppressed by the devil. (See Isaiah 61:1 and Luke 4:18.) God gave us the Holy Spirit so we could minister miracles to those around us. We need to be just as "sticky" about giving miracles as we are about receiving them.

COMPLEMENT, DON'T COMPETE

We know that God uses different people to minister in different ways. Elijah ministered in miracles of judgment, but Elisha ministered in miracles of mercy. Elijah came from a simple, rural background, and Elisha came from a very wealthy background. Elijah lived alone in caves and ravens fed him. Elisha lived with people and had servants. Elijah was taken to heaven in a whirlwind, and Elisha died a natural death: two mighty men of God, both of whom walked in the miraculous, but who were as different as night and day.

Now I am going to tell you something. Every one of us is going to minister differently in the miraculous. When we expect to agree on everything and behave the same way, then we get into all kinds of trouble. Haven't you heard that phrase, "different strokes for different folks." Well, it's the same thing in ministering to people. We're not all going to do things the same way.

Ministering in miracles isn't limited just to the "biggies" like healing, finances, etc. Someone in the choir may minister a miracle in song. A person with the motive gift of helps might bless the church and, in doing so, give a miracle. I might pray for a miracle for someone by laying my hands on them. Another person might pray for a miracle and never touch them. When we find our own unique ministries, then we can begin to flow in miracles.

I counted once and discovered that Happy

Church, the church my husband Wally pastors in Denver, Colorado, has many different ministries. That means many different categories of people are being served by the church. Now if we're all competing against each other and judging one another for our differences, then we wouldn't have miracles here; we would have knock-down, drag-out fights. We would be *competing* rather than *complementing*.

Moses didn't beat Joshua over the head because he had a different ministry. Abraham didn't forsake Lot, even though Lot was off in left field sometimes. I don't get up and leave the sanctuary because someone else is signing to the deaf or singing a solo. Our likeness and differences *together* make the picture complete. We need to let the Holy Spirit flow in each of us in order to experience miracles.

THE CALL
TO MINISTER

Do you know that God will call you to the ministry and put you where He wants you? If you hate to sing in the choir, God is not going to call you to a music ministry. If little kids are not your thing, God will not call you to be the director of the preschool program. God is very practical. He knows your strengths and weaknesses, and He doesn't want to highlight your weaknesses!

One time a woman came up to me at a convention and told me something very unusual. She said God had told her to leave her family and move to Denver to live with me. She said I was to train her for her ministry and be a mentor to her. I found out that on a certain date she would arrive in town, and I was to pick her up at the airlines at a certain time.

You can imagine how I was feeling at that particular time. I would have laughed except this woman was very serious. I didn't want to discourage her, but I had to tell her that God hadn't shared this news with me. If God had wanted us to work together, He would have told me too. God is not impolite and rude!

As I talked with this woman, I told her I believed God had a call on her life but that this particular situation was not of God. I prayed with her that God would reveal His perfect plan to her and that her ministry would be very special. She didn't get angry or uptight with me, and she seemed to understand what I was saying to her.

Sometimes the call to a ministry comes suddenly, but you just know that it is God. Other times the call starts out as a small seed, and it grows very slowly. But you still know that it is God speaking to you. When God tells you what to do and when, then your ministry will be successful and full of miracles.

TIMES
OF TRIAL

Walking in the miraculous is the best place to be. Whether you are receiving a miracle for yourself or ministering a miracle to someone else, seeing the supernatural is wonderful. But I wouldn't be telling the truth if I didn't say there would be some real times of testing. The devil will try to get you to give up before the harvest of your miracle ever comes. If you are in the ministry, people will laugh at you and criticize your work. You'll start on a project and it will fall apart; you'll lay hands on someone for healing, and nothing will happen. Your finances will be attacked along with your health and your family. The devil will fight tooth and nail to keep you from the miraculous.

When times of trial come, what should you do? Lay down and quit? Give up on your miracle? Stop ministering? No! You hang on until that miracle comes. You may have to fast for ten days and pray four hours a day. But if you hang in with God, He will hang in with you.

Elisha knew that his call was to walk in the miraculous. He also knew that Elijah had something he needed, and Elisha wasn't going to let Elijah go to heaven until he had it. Right before Elijah was to be caught up to heaven, he said to Elisha:

> *". . . Tarry here, I pray thee; for the LORD hath sent me to Bethel . . . "*
> (II Kings 2:2).

Now here is a testing. Elijah tells Elisha to stay behind, but Elisha wants the double portion. Elisha could have given up on his miracle and said, "Okay, whatever you say." But instead Elisha said: *"As the Lord liveth, and as thy soul liveth, I will not leave thee."* Elisha was going to stick to Elijah no matter what. Well, several more times Elijah tried to get Elisha to stay behind, but it didn't work. Finally, Elijah asked Elisha what it was he wanted:

> *And it came to pass, when they were gone over, that Elijah said unto Elisha, Ask what I shall do for thee, before I be taken away from thee. And Elisha said, I pray thee, let a double portion of thy spirit be upon me. And he* [Elijah] *said, Thou hast asked a hard thing: nevertheless, if thou see me when I am taken from thee, it shall be so unto thee; but if not, it shall not be so* (II Kings 2:9,10).

Elisha wanted the mantle of Elijah so he could walk in the miraculous. Elisha diligently watched;

and suddenly, as Elijah was caught away, Elisha saw the mantle of Elijah. Elisha tore his own clothes off and put on the mantle of Elijah. He had received the double portion; and, from this point, Elisha walked in the miraculous.

I don't ever plan to fail, and I don't want you to fail either. Every Christian should expect the supernatural in their lives and in their ministries. The Holy Spirit of God was made to be our mantle, and we need to be looking for miracles. Now repeat this after me:

"My foundation is built on the Word of God. I speak the words of Jesus and not the words of the devil. I act like a winner because Jesus is a winner. My mind is renewed to the Word of Truth which can set me free from failure. I am a 'sticky' Christian because I will not give up on my miracle. I have the mantle of the Holy Spirit; and, therefore, I can minister miracles to people around me. I will not give up in times of trials because I serve a supernatural God! No defeat or lie of the devil will ever rob me of a miracle because Jesus lives big in me, amen."

Now go out and get your miracle today!

Chapter Four

MIRACLES FOR MATERIAL FAMINE

One of the most startling things you notice when you visit a famine-stricken land is the plight of the people. Their bellies are bloated from lack of food, and their skin is yellowed from vitamin deficiency. Sometimes they are blind because of malnutrition, and disease is widespread. Starvation kills children daily as they lie in their mother's arms. You cannot help but feel overwhelmed with sorrow when you are in these surroundings.

When we think of famines, we usually think of starving people in far-away drought-ridden lands. We're so blessed to live in America where famine and starvation are almost an unknown thing. However, famines aren't always related to crops and drought and starving people. Famines can occur in other areas too; such as, financial famines, material famines, spiritual famines, and health famines. Anytime the devil gets ahold of an area of our lives and causes a great shortage or lack, there is a famine.

GOD WANTS US BLESSED.

You know, when God put people on the earth, He didn't say, "Well, I hope you make it all right down there. It's going to be rough at times, but don't talk to me about it because you're on your own." God is a loving and gentle God. He doesn't throw us to the wolves to see if we'll make it. He is concerned with every detail of our lives, and that includes our health, our families, our jobs, our finances, and our interests. God purposely didn't make robots—He made real people because He is real. God also has real miracles to help us during our famine times.

Long before the devil got the lease on this earth, God planned for His creation to be prosperous. That meant He wanted man to have soul prosperity, health prosperity, and material prosperity. God wanted His creation to be successful and to flourish because He was successful and flourishing. You have heard the expression, "Like father, like son"? It is the same way with God. Since everything God does prospers, then He wants the same to be true for His children. God is not a God of lack and despair.

But when the devil deceived Adam and Eve and caused them to fall into sin, the earth fell out of God's control and into the devil's control. The devil became the god of this world, and in essence, all creation became like him. Where there was health, there became sickness and disease. Where there was joy, there became sorrow and travail. Where there was wealth and prosperity, there became poverty and defeat.

Now this would be a pretty grim story if I stopped here, but I have good news. The devil may be a god of lack, but God is a God of abundance! When you were born again and switched *daddys*, you came to the God that owns the whole earth and everything in it. Your daddy in heaven is not stingy or cheap. When He makes a sunset, He doesn't use some old and faded, hand-me-down watercolors. He uses the finest paints on the market. Likewise, when you have a material need, God isn't going to give you a hand-me-down miracle that will barely get you through. You're going to see a miracle that will catch the eyes of the world. If you think that FTD does a good job delivering the best, then just wait until you see what God has in store to bless you!

WEALTHY AND HEALTHY

Today we see Christians living in poverty because they believe that it is God's will for their lives. They have been taught that money is evil and that it brings more hardship than good. But we know this is not true because the Bible shows us many examples of people who had an abundance of material possessions, and yet were very godly.

Job was one of the wealthiest men ever to live on the earth:

> *And there were born unto him seven*
> *sons and three daughters. His*

substance also was seven thousand sheep, and three thousand camels, and five hundred yoke of oxen, and five hundred she asses, and a very great household; so that this man was the greatest of all the men of the east (Job 1:2,3).

Now when the devil came to accuse Job before God, do you think God said: "Satan, you are right to accuse this man because, after all, he is so prosperous and well-to-do. It makes me sick to see him with all this wealth. He should be poor so that he would love Me more and serve Me better." That was what the devil *wanted* to hear!

But you and I know that wasn't what really happened. Here is what God said to the devil:

. . . Hast thou considered my servant Job, that there is none like him in the earth, a perfect and an upright man, one that feareth God, and escheweth evil? (Job 1:8).

God called Job a perfect man. If it was wrong to be wealthy and prosperous, do you think God would have described Job this way? No! God knew that Job had a heart for the things of God. Job sought after soul prosperity first and got blessed with material prosperity as a bonus.

Abraham was also very well-to-do. He had lots of cattle and land and was a wise merchant.

Sarah had dresses in all the latest styles with matching accessories and shoes; and, her hair was done every week. Because Abraham was blessed so was his wife! But Abraham's prosperity didn't happen because of luck. His success came because he had a heart for God first and not a heart for money.

I used to think that if I were wealthy my money would probably drive me away from God. "If I had lots of money," I reasoned, "I wouldn't need God because money would solve my problems." Then I found out that having money wasn't the problem—it was the love of money that was the problem. First Timothy 6:10 says that the love of money is the root of all evil. I heard a good example once that really helped me to understand this scripture. There were two men walking down the street, one with two cents in his pocket and one with two million dollars in his pocket. Money consumed the thoughts of both of these men. They each had the same problem: money was their god. It doesn't matter how much or how little you have in the bank; if money becomes more important than serving the Lord, then money has become your god.

One time Wally bought me a beautiful string of pearls for Valentine's Day. I was just convinced that having those pearls was evil and wrong, and I was really upset with Wally. But then my mother gave me some wise counsel. Thank God for mothers! She told me to thank God that my husband loved me enough to buy me pearls, and to receive them as a blessing from the Lord. Those few words really helped me. I learned that God wanted to bless me materially through my husband, and that wasn't evil!

OVERCOMING THE GREAT FAMINE

So many times when we are faced with difficult financial situations, we feel that our problems must be the worst in the history of mankind. But I want us to look at a horrible circumstance in II Kings 6 where God absolutely brought a miracle of material wealth. Hold on to your stomachs because this is strong stuff:

> *And it came to pass after this, that Benhadad king of Syria gathered all his host, and went up, and besieged Samaria. And there was a great famine in Samaria: and, behold, they besieged it, until an ass's head was sold for fourscore pieces of silver, and the fourth part of a cab of dove's dung for five pieces of silver. And as the king of Israel was passing by upon the wall, there cried a woman unto him, saying,*

Help, my lord, O king. And he said,
If the LORD do not help thee, whence
shall I help thee? out of the barn floor,
or out of the winepress? And the king
said unto her, What aileth thee? And
she answered, This woman said unto
me, Give thy son, that we may eat him
to day, and we will eat my son tomor-
row. So we boiled my son, and did eat
him: and I said unto her on the next
day, Give thy son, that we may eat
him: and she hath hid her son
(II Kings 6:24-29).

The famine is so terrible that the people are literally starving to death. The city of Samaria was surrounded on every side by Benhadad's armies. No one could enter or leave the city. Because the people were desperate, they were boiling their own children and eating them. You're thinking, "Marilyn, this is so disgusting." I know it is. But in a few moments, it will get better.

THE CURSE CAUSELESS SHALL NOT COME.

Bad situations are cursed situations. Sin, sickness, disease, and poverty are all results of the curses that come because of sin. There are curses that result from sexual sin, idolatry, and rebellion—just to name a few. Curses are birthed from sin and disobedience; and, they bring death into a situation.

The Bible has something interesting to say about the occurrence of curses. Proverbs 26:2 says: *"... the curse causeless shall not come."* A curse can't come upon a nation or a person without a reason. If you are into sexual sin, then a curse is upon your life. If you cheat the company by embezzling money, then you are into sin and disobedience; and a curse will come.

Now there are some Christians who think they can get by with sin and not pay any consequences. They may say, "It doesn't really matter if I don't tithe because that's an Old Testament teaching, and we're in the New Testament days. Besides, I need this money more than the church does. Have you seen the way the pastor dresses? Have you noticed all the shoes his wife owns? What about that fancy car they drive? Why, they don't need my money!" Curses don't come without a reason folks.

Why has this terrible curse—this famine— come upon Israel? Let's look at the king for a moment. His name is Jehoram (remember, he was the king who wanted to attack Moab in our first lesson), and he was an evil man. His father was Ahab and his mother was Jezebel; actually, the whole family was nothing but thugs. Jehoram led the nation of Israel into idolatry by worshiping golden calves. The *curse causeless* cannot come, but if idolatry is your thing, then here comes the curse.

FAILING TO BELIEVE GOD

The first part of the curse was the attack by the army of Syria. Syria's king, Benhadad, said, "We're going to take over Israel once and for all, and make it ours." Now Benhadad wasn't too swift; he had seen the results of miracle after miracle and he still refused to repent and serve God. (Jehoram had also seen some miracles, but he wasn't too swift either.) Benhadad no doubt knew that Naaman, his military leader, was healed from leprosy, and still he refused to believe. In fact, Benhadad gave Naaman permission to go to Elisha for a miracle. Remember when Elisha raised the Shunammite's son from the dead? Benhadad later met the risen boy and his mother. See, God put him in situations where he could be delivered from curses. But the old king just loved to sin, and he was determined to disobey God and capture Israel anyway.

I know some Christians that must be related to Benhadad. They see miracle after miracle, but their hearts don't change. They whine, "I know that so-and-so was healed of cancer, but it won't happen for me! Healing isn't for everyone you know!" *Pop, goes the miracle.* Instead of getting a wonderful deliverance, some people just stay in rebellion and live out their curse.

You have to step out and believe God for your miracle. If you are in a cursed situation, then you have to ask God for help. He doesn't get mad if He has to answer questions, because He loves to teach you to win. If you don't know how a curse came to your family, ask God; He will tell you. If you are living in sin, the Holy Spirit will reveal your sin and help you clean up your act. Curses bring death, but miracles bring life. The Bible says to choose life!

SACKCLOTH AND ASHES

When Jehoram heard that people were eating their children because the famine was so severe, he got very angry:

> *And it came to pass, when the king heard the words of the woman, that he rent his clothes; and he passed by upon the wall, and the people looked, and, behold, he had sackcloth within upon his flesh* (II Kings 6:30).

Jehoram was really ticked off with the situation. He knew who to blame for this mess. Elisha, that's who. Elisha's prayers had brought this problem:

Then he said, God do so and more also to me, if the head of Elisha the son of Shaphat shall stand on him this day (II Kings 6:31).

It is so easy to blame others for our sins. We hear the Word of Truth which can change our lives, but we don't put it into practice. We grumble, "I know I should tithe, but everything in my house is falling apart. The bill collectors are knocking at my door, and my car won't run. I can't afford to tithe." As the situation gets worse and worse, so does our attitude. "If so-and-so hadn't said I could be prosperous, then I wouldn't have these troubles anyway. I'm never going to that church again!" Blaming others for our problems can be the easy way out.

God wants us to examine our lives by examining our motives and actions. Jehoram was mad because he knew he had blown it. Elisha was the example of the truth, and Jehoram couldn't stand it. He wanted Elisha dead so he would feel better about his sin. Do you remember when David committed adultery with Bathsheba, and then killed her husband Uriah? His sin of adultery was too much to bear, so he killed Uriah to try to cover his sin and make things right again for himself. But the curse came, and David lost his firstborn son of Bathsheba. Sin doesn't pay in any form or shape. Never let things go from bad to worse. Instead, repent and ask God for a turn-around. Ask Him to help turn your *sackcloth and ashes* into *miracles and peace*.

WINDOWS IN HEAVEN

Elisha knew what was going on in the city, but he wasn't nervous. He wasn't sitting at home, biting his nails, having a pity party, and fretting that there wasn't any food. Elisha had seen enough miracles in his life to know that God was faithful to His Word and that a turnaround was just around the corner. Elisha wasn't trusting in that stupid King Jehoram or that dummy Benhadad who worshipped pomegranates. (Syria's idol was a pomegranate.) Elisha knew that the living God was his source.

So here we can visualize Elisha patiently sitting with his elders as they wait for God to speak. Elisha didn't jump out and say, "God, in case you didn't know, we have a very serious problem here in the land. We need to get going on this because I am getting nervous." Elisha's elders weren't criticizing him and telling him to get a move on with the famine problem. Everyone was trusting the Lord God of Israel. They were in one accord—waiting for God's plan of action.

LIGHT IS GREATER
THAN DARKNESS.

When "famines" occur in our material needs, the first thing we like to do is talk about the problem. We tell our neighbors and friends all about our terrible money problems. We get out of faith and into foolishness, and then we really have difficulties. We start to blame God, our spouses, our children, our pastors, and probably our dogs. But did you know that talking about our problems brings death? That's right, *death*. And death brings total darkness to our situations. Living in the dark keeps us from the truth. But the Bible says Jesus is the Light of the whole world. If we keep our eyes focused on Him during our financial famines, then Jesus will penetrate the darkness with the truth of the Word.

You know, electricity is an amazing thing. It has so much power, yet it can be channeled into just the right place at the right time. When we want light in our bedrooms, we turn on the switch and instantly we have light. Because the power of electricity was channeled through the wires to that switch, when we touched the switch, light appeared through the elements of the light bulb.

If there is a financial famine in your house, Jesus is ready to pour on the power! We can simply say, "Jesus, I have a great need here in my life. I'm in a cursed place, and I need a miracle to get me on my feet again." Jesus loves this kind of prayer. He is the power source of your miracle. He can bring His power to "turn on the switch" and bring light to the problem. You may think that your problem is unique in all the world, and it may be. However, Jesus can channel His power directly to your need and instantly take you from the cursed place into the "promised land"!

I have purposed to be like Elisha and run with the winners who believe that God will bring in the people by the thousands. I'm not going to sit in the darkness and talk about all the problems that want to block this goal. Jesus is my power source, and I want Him to be such a great light in my life that people will see that light in the midst of their own darkness. Hurting people will know that *my* God is a God of miracles!

PROCLAIM WHAT GOD CAN DO.

Finally, Elisha heard the Word of the Lord; and, he proclaimed it to the people:

> . . . *Thus saith the LORD, To morrow about this time shall a measure of fine flour be sold for a shekel, and two measures of barley for a shekel, in the*

80

gate of Samaria (II Kings 7:1).

Here we have some really tremendous news from the voice of God. Tomorrow there will be food in the land! Now if you were starving, wouldn't this be good news to you? Wouldn't you want to dance a little jig right there in the street? *Food is coming tomorrow!* What glorious news!

Now Elisha wasn't making up this story. He had heard from the Lord, and he boldly proclaimed the news to the people. But wouldn't you know, in the midst of such wonderful news, there is a servant of the king who doesn't believe Elisha:

> *Then a lord on whose hand the king*
> *leaned answered the man of God, and*
> *said, Behold, if the LORD would make*
> *windows in heaven, might this thing*
> *be? . . .* (II Kings 7:2).

This servant with the king didn't believe Elisha. "Oh, come on Elisha! There isn't a morsel of food in sight, and you say we will be buying food tomorrow? Why, God would have to make windows in heaven and drop all that food here in order for this thing to happen. Really, Elisha, get with the program."

This attitude of the king's servant is just like the attitude of some Christians. They hear the Word of God, and they reject it because they don't believe God is a God of miracles. God wanted to do a miracle for Israel—and even for the king's servant. But they were in doubt and unbelief, so God couldn't send the miracle. Remember when we talked about miracles being faith seeds? Well, if you have doubt and unbelief seeds, you won't get a miracle because there is no life in you. Miracles grow from faith seeds that have been activated in our hearts by the living Word of God.

So here we have a doubter in the midst of a miracle. The doubter doesn't believe that God can bring light into the situation and reverse the curse. He thinks that God will have to open the windows of heaven in order for anything to happen. Elisha knew that God was going to open the windows of heaven and bring the miracle, because God *does* open the windows of heaven to bless us. In Malachi 3 we read:

> *Bring ye all the tithes into the storehouse, that there may be meat in mine house, and prove me now herewith, saith the LORD of hosts, if I will not open you the windows of heaven, and pour you out a blessing, that there shall not be room enough to receive it. And I will rebuke the devourer for your sakes, and he shall not destroy the fruits of your ground; neither shall your vine cast her fruit before the time in the field, saith the LORD of hosts* (Malachi 3:10-11).

When we are faithful to tithe, even in the midst of a financial famine in our home, God has promised to open the windows of heaven and pour out a blessing in our lives. He will bring the miraculous into our famine and cause money to come to us in every direction. "Well," you say, "but what if God doesn't know to send us money?" God knows *exactly* what you need before you even ask Him. He won't send you a year's supply of chocolate if you need money. He will open the windows of heaven and give you the means to obtain money, or He will move supernaturally on someone's heart to give you money.

I have heard of people who have tithed their last cent; and, within a few days, some rich aunt calls them up asking if they could use some money. There have been cases where business people have been in a real slump in their sales; and after beginning to tithe, their sales increased 100 percent. God wants you to be a success.

Well, you say, "Yes, but I tithe all the time and I still have money problems." It's important to know that we're all in a battle. Maybe we stand firm for a little while, but then we give up on our miracle. Or maybe we doubt God like the servant. But we must all put on our spiritual boxing gloves and be famine fighters. The devil has stolen from you, and you need to keep hitting that rat with the Word of God until the famine is broken. We are to proclaim the Word of the Lord until we see it manifested in our lives.

DOERS OF THE WORD

There are times when we want to lie down and hibernate until our financial situations change. We get "down and out" and discouraged by the lack in our lives. We reason away our miracle and live in a famine-stricken land filled with doubt and unbelief. The darkness becomes greater than the light, and the windows in heaven seem to be temporarily "out of order."

But did you know that God's miracle supply never runs out? His storehouse of blessings doesn't go on vacation four times a year. God is always ready to help us out in our time of famine. But, sometimes His method of helping us might be a little peculiar:

> *And there were four leprous men at the entering in of the gate: and they said one to another, Why sit we here until we die? If we say, We will enter into the city, then the famine is in the city, and we shall die there: and if we sit still here, we die also. Now therefore come, and let us fall unto the host of the Syrians: if they save us alive, we shall live; and if they kill us, we shall but die* (II Kings 7:3-4).

These four lepers had made a major decision. If they sat outside the gate, they were going to die. If they went inside the gate (which they weren't allowed to do because they were "unclean") and into the city, they would die also. Either way, there was no food and death was a certainty.

THE GUTS TO GET OUT OF RUTS

So these men became bold and said, "Hey, we don't care if we look funny because the leprosy has eaten away our flesh. We are going to take a big chance here and see if the Syrians will take us in and feed us. If they will, then we won't die of starvation. If they say, 'Sorry, people without noses aren't allowed in the city,' then we will accept that and die. We must take a chance—because doing something is better than waiting to die."

These men got out their walking sticks and headed for the Syrian camp. They were so hungry and tired, yet they had a hope that kept them going. They had the guts to get out of ruts!

The closer they got to the camp, the more they noticed how quiet it seemed. Nobody was even watching the gate. So they walked into the camp and guess who they saw? Nobody. That's right,

85

nobody. The only thing that they saw was lots of food. They ran over and began to eat, eat, and eat. They were so hungry that they didn't even count their calories. This was simply wonderful—all kinds of food around and nobody to bother them.

Where do you suppose the Syrians were that day? Let's read the Word and find out what had happened:

> *For the Lord had made the host of the Syrians to hear a noise of chariots, and a noise of horses, even the noise of a great host: and they said one to another, Lo, the king of Israel hath hired against us the kings of the Hittites, and the kings of the Egyptians, to come upon us. Wherefore they arose and fled in the twilight, and left their tents, and their horses, and their asses, even the camp as it was, and fled for their life* (II Kings 7:6-7).

Here we see the miracle God had performed. He caused the Syrians to hear a great noise that sounded like thousands of men and horses rushing toward the city. The first thing the Syrians thought was that Jehoram had gotten the Hittites and the Egyptians, which were the two largest armies in the area, to come and attack them. They became so terrified that they fled for their lives and left all their material possessions in the camp.

When the lepers came into the camp, they had found an abundance of food and material wealth just sitting there for the taking. First, they had eaten, then they had tried on clothes. One of them said, "Look at this gorgeous outfit. I may have leprosy, but this is certainly my color." On and on they went, eating and admiring the wealth of the Syrians. Finally, though, one of them said, "Hey, don't you think we should go back and tell the people of Israel that we have found food? Let's share our blessings with everyone else at home."

OPENING THE GATES
OF BLESSING

So the lepers went back into the city. Their bellies were fat, they had barbecued-rib breath, and they were burping. One had on designer pants and another had on a fur coat. They cried out to the people, "The Syrian army is gone! Come and see all the food that they left! And all the clothes and jewelry and money! Hurry! Go to the camp and eat!"

You can imagine what the city people must have thought while listening and looking at the four lepers. It certainly didn't take much convincing to see that the lepers weren't lying. The people could see the new clothes; they could hear the burps; they could smell the food on their breath:

> *And the people went out, and spoiled the tents of the Syrians. So a measure of fine flour was sold for a shekel, and two measures of barley for a shekel, according to the word of the LORD. And the king appointed the lord on whose hand he leaned to have the charge of the gate: and the people trode upon him in the gate, and he died, as the man of God had said, who spake when the king came down to him* (II Kings 7:16-17).

The people of Israel raced to the Syrian camp. They were all trying to get in at once because they were starved. Now remember the servant who didn't believe Elisha's prophecy? Elisha had told him that he could see the wealth and the food but that he wouldn't partake of it. Well, the king told the servant to help the crowd get through the gate in an orderly manner. But these people were wild with hunger. So when the servant opened the gate, suddenly hundreds of people come rushing toward him. He couldn't get out of the way in time—and crunch—the hungry mob trampled him and that was the end. He died just as Elisha had said.

TAKING THE SPOIL

We see in this lesson that God had a plan for the people of Israel. He spoke through his prophet Elisha and told him that there would be food. The curse was being reversed because the people were turning back to God.

You can either believe God for miracles or you can be like the king's servant. He doubted God and mocked Elisha, and as a result, he died just at the dawning of the promise of hope.

You've got to have guts to get out of ruts. Christians need to stand up and say, "The world says to do things this way, but I choose to serve God." When you make a decision to be gutsy with God, He will open the windows of heaven and bring you your financial miracle. The gate of blessing will swing open as you obey God, and there will be abundance and not lack. We are the chosen people of God. We're supposed to take the spoil and be filled to our heart's content.

Now I want you to say this with me:

"I will overcome my financial famine.

I will not allow the curse causeless to come.

I will allow the Holy Spirit to clean me up so I can walk free from curses.

I will believe God to meet my needs.

I will exchange my sackcloth and ashes for miracles and peace.

I will give to God and expect the windows of heaven to open for me.

I will walk in the light and not in the darkness.

I will proclaim what God can and will do in my life.

I will have the guts to get out of ruts.

I will open the gates of God's kingdom and live in prosperity.

I will take the spoil from the devil and claim my miracle.''

Reach out and grab your miracle of abundance today; and, stomp out that material famine in the name of Jesus!

Chapter Five
FIRST-FRUIT MIRACLES

On almost any newsstand today you will see several different magazines and newspapers dealing with financial matters. We have the *Wall Street Journal*, *Forbes*, *Money*, and *Consumer Report*, just to name a few. Most of the articles within these publications focus on making good investments, getting the proper tax shelters, selecting sound IRA plans, and avoiding financial catastrophes. All around us we see what money can buy: beautiful homes, luxurious cruises, imported clothes, and fancy cars. But in the midst of all this, there is one thing we don't see. We don't see God's plan for financial and material success. The world does not operate on God's financial plan, and we know that anything that is not of God cannot ultimately be successful. Wouldn't it be a wonderful thing to open the *Wall Street Journal* and see a section on how to prosper according to God's Word?

Because Satan is the god of this world, people today are mixed up about their financial matters. But God has given us some guidelines to help us make wise decisions. How many of you know that God is very practical? He is concerned with money and how it comes and goes. The Bible has a lot to say about money and working and planning ahead, so we aren't left in the dark. God hasn't "left us guessing" and, therefore, vulnerable to ghastly mistakes. No! He has made a way for us to prosper and succeed without any sorrow and worry attached.

GOD IS NOT
A PUSHOVER

Have you seen the television commercial about Morris the cat? Well, Morris has a real problem in his life: he is a finicky eater. That's right, he picks at his food and he won't touch new things. He likes the same old thing every day. If you try to give him something new or different, he sniffs indignantly and refuses even to taste it!

You say, "Marilyn, what has this to do with my relationship with God?" Let me tell you. There are a lot of Christians who are finicky with God. They pick at the Bible and pull out of it what they want. "Oh, I know that the Bible says not to gossip, but I'm not *really* hurting anybody!" "Sure, the Bible says to go to church, but I don't like other Christians, so I'm going to stay home and watch TV instead." "I know I should tithe, but it's no big deal. Besides, some rich person will give my portion anyway." Like Morris, we don't like to have our lifestyles altered. We get into a comfortable rut and changing seems to be too much effort. "You want me to do what? Pray with you at 7:00 tomorrow morning at the church? Oh, I couldn't do *that*, I really need my sleep!" You may think that you can cover up God's eyes and live any way you want, but I have news for you: God is *not* a pushover! He can't tolerate sin any better today than He could 2000 years ago. Sin is a disgrace to any people, and we'll soon see how a finicky nation almost collapsed because of its rebellious ways.

RAIN, RAIN, GO AWAY

We've been studying a lot about Elijah and Elisha, and how God used them to deliver both judgment and mercy to the nation of Israel. We know that the Israelites were very hard-hearted during this time and turned their backs on God to worship idols. Men and women would worship everything from stars to golden images—even to *pomegranates*. At first, I couldn't believe that anyone would be foolish enough to worship a pomegranate! But I found out that Naaman worshipped a pomegranate idol called Nisrock. Can you imagine getting up in the morning and thanking a pomegranate for the day? Only God is worthy of our praise.

In Elijah's day Israel was a very rebellious and evil nation led by none other than Ahab and Jezebel. The Bible says that Ahab did more to provoke God than all the other kings before him, so we know Ahab wasn't too swift. Elijah came along and began his ministry by pronouncing judgment on the nation:

*And Elijah the Tishbite, . . . said unto
Ahab, As the LORD God of Israel
liveth, before whom I stand, there shall
not be dew nor rain these years, but
according to my word* (I Kings 17:1).

God became angry with Israel and its sin, so He closed up the heavens. For three-and-a-half years not a drop of rain fell to the ground! We know that without rain crops can't grow; and if we don't have crops, we don't have food. So the result was a famine that spread throughout Israel.

Three-and-a-half years later, Elijah called the people of God together along with the prophets of Baal. He said there was going to be a sacrifice to prove who was the real God of Israel. Was it going to be Baal or Jehovah God? Whichever answered by fire would be the one true God. So the prophets of Baal called on their god to rain down fire:

*And they cried aloud, and cut
themselves after their manner with
knives and lancets, till the blood
gushed out upon them. And it came to
pass, when midday was past, and they
prophesied until the time of the offering
of the evening sacrifice, that there was
neither voice, nor any to answer, nor*

any that regarded (I Kings 18:28-29).

The prophets of Baal had carried on for hours, and still their god hadn't appeared. Elijah had to fix the altar of the Lord before he could offer the sacrifice! But now watch what happened. At the time of the evening sacrifice, Elijah called upon God to rain down fire upon the altar. Sure enough, down came the fire, and the people fell on their faces and repented of their sins. God then opened the heavens, and rain fell once again on the earth.

Now Elisha didn't have to deal with Ahab because he was dead. But he had to deal with another thug Jehoram who was Ahab and Jezebel's son. Jehoram was an evil man, and he led the people of Israel into idolatry. Once again, the people turned away from God, got rebellious in their ways, and a famine developed.

We know that there was a great famine in the land because, once again, the people had turned from the living God. We also know from a prior chapter that the famine would become so severe that people would eat their own children in order to survive. The nation was really suffering because of its sinful ways, yet the people continued to worship graven images and other idols instead of Jehovah God.

Remember, God is not a pushover. You can't be an ''on again off again'' Christian. The Bible is not a light switch you turn on or turn off at will. You can't be finicky and only take from the Bible what you think will be easy for you. If you don't watch it, you will end up with some sort of famine in your own life. I know that sounds rough and tough, but that's Bible, folks. God wants all of you and not just part of you. When you seek Him first, your soul begins to prosper and then comes the material and financial prosperity.

A HEART FOR GOD

But, in the midst of this agonizing situation, came a man who had a heart for God. Now we don't know this man's name but we know he was from a town called Baal-shalisha. Baal-shalisha was named by Jezebel when she was queen. The original name of the town was Shalisha, but Jezebel loved Baal so much that she wanted to change all the names of the cities to include the name Baal. So Shalisha became Baal-shalisha according to Jezebel's wishes.

This man from Baal-shalisha had been enrolled in Elisha's Bible school, and he knew of God's prosperity system. When his harvest season came, he did something very unusual for that particular time in Israel:

> *And there came a man from Baal-shalisha, and brought the man of God*

bread of the firstfruits, twenty loaves of barley, and full ears of corn in the husk thereof. And he said, Give unto the people, that they may eat (II Kings 4:42).

This man gave of his first fruits from his harvest. Now remember, it's slim picking in Israel. Food was hard to get, and most people were taking what little food they had and hiding it from each other. But here was a man who really had a heart for God. He knew the blessing was in the giving and not in the keeping. So he came to Elisha and gave him the first fruit of his crops and said, "Here, take this food and give it to the hungry people."

I really admire this man because he reached out for a miracle during some really desperate times. He could have kept that food for himself and perhaps for his family. But he put God first so he could receive a miracle. The devil probably came to him and taunted, "You are one big sucker for doing this you know. You are going to starve now because you gave your food away. God isn't going to come down here and feed you, so you just wasted your time, buddy." The man's faith was challenged. The circumstances looked bad. Sense knowledge told him to take what he had and run because the famine was simply awful. But this faithful man didn't let the circumstances stop him from reaching for a miracle. He gave in order to receive.

We, too, can get into some really tight situations. Financially, it can look so awful that we want to bury our heads in the sand and forget everything. But this is the time we should examine our hearts and decide which way we are going to go. Will we go God's way? or the devil's way? Will we give our first fruits to God? or will we keep them for ourselves?

The Bible has a lot to say about giving our first fruits—our tithes and offerings. The world's system says "Take, so you can get." The Bible says, "Give, so you can receive." There is a sharp contrast between the ways of God and the ways of the devil. At times it almost seems foolish to give our money away when we so desperately need it. But God's ways are the right ways, no matter what our heads tell us. In order to receive, we have to give God something with which to work.

Deuteronomy 12:11 says:

> *Then there shall be a place which the LORD your God shall choose to cause his name to dwell there; thither shall ye bring all that I command you; your burnt offerings, and your sacrifices, your tithes, and the heave offering of your hand, and all your choice vows which ye vow unto the LORD.*

God commanded the people during the Old Testament times to tithe to Him. God wasn't after their money: He was after their hearts. The heart of man is such an interesting thing: it can be full of evil or full of righteousness. Out of it can come blessings or cursings. Giving of your first fruits changes your heart and helps you develop a godly attitude of generosity and giving. When God has your heart, He will also have your pocketbook!

When we bring our first fruits into God's storehouse, the Word says God will *open* the windows of heaven, not close them. Rebellious hearts and stingy attitudes close up the heavens, and our miracles never come. But hearts that are open to God also open the avenue for blessings and miracles. A generous person who not only gives to God but to others will be blessed in all he does. Tithing is a spiritual principle that causes blessings to chase us and miracles to surround us!

So we've looked at a man who had a generous and giving heart. He gave willingly of his first fruits so that others would be refreshed. I know in my heart that this man received some tremendous miracles because of his act of obedience. He received some first-fruit miracles because of the attitude of his heart and his obedience to the Word.

SPIRITUAL ACTION = SPIRITUAL REACTION

There are a lot of Christians today who are in the "name it and claim it" club. Now don't misunderstand—God wants you to tell Him about your needs and desires:

> *Be careful for nothing; but in every thing by prayer and supplication with thanksgiving let your requests be made known unto God* (Philippians 4:6).

God is not a scrooge. He wants you to be blessed in all areas, especially your finances. But a lot of Christians are in need of major "heart surgery." They are finicky and really don't have a heart for God. They don't give of their first fruits, and then they wonder why everything is going from bad to worse. Let me tell you that any kind of spiritual action leads to a spiritual reaction. If you sow sparingly, you reap sparingly. If you give generously, you reap generously. If you are rebellious, then you can expect a famine in your life. Spiritual matters are not just toys we can play with and discard when we get tired of them. We need to get serious with God so that He can be serious with us.

EVIL HEART
OF UNBELIEF

I want to tell you about a man who had some major "heart problems." His name was Gehazi, and he was the servant of Elisha. Now you would think that since Gehazi was with Elisha night and day, he should have been pretty swift. Well, he was not swift at all because his heart was not right with God.

Gehazi was with Elisha when the man from Baal-shalisha came with his first fruits. Instead of seeing the potential for a miracle from the giving of the food, Gehazi was disgusted:

> *And his servitor said, What, should I
> set this before an hundred men? He
> [Elisha] said again, Give the people,
> that they may eat: for thus saith the
> LORD, They shall eat, and shall leave
> thereof* (II Kings 4:43).

Gehazi's problem was that he had an evil heart:

> *A good man out of the good treasure
> of the heart bringeth forth good
> things: and an evil man out of the evil
> treasure bringeth forth evil things*
> (Matthew 12:35).

Elisha had already told Gehazi to give the people the food. Gehazi looked at the amount of food and the amount of the people and said, "What? Are you kidding? There isn't enough food here to feed all these people? Why even bother?" Gehazi's heart was full of unbelief, and he doubted the power of God to multiply the food.

Does this story sound familiar to another story in the Bible? Remember the disciple Philip and his reaction to the two fish and five loaves of bread? He looked at the small amount of food compared with the huge amount of people, and he said it was impossible. How could two fish and five loaves of bread possibly feed five thousand people? Philip had a "heart problem" just like Gehazi did.

WISE HEARTS
GUIDE OUR MOUTHS

Gehazi has been a problem to me for a long time. Although he hung around with one of the most outstanding men of God ever to live on the earth, he remained *full* of unbelief. Let me tell you one of the great miracles that involved Gehazi:

> *And it fell on a day, that Elisha passed*
> *to Shunem, where was a great woman;*
> *and she constrained him to eat bread.*
> *And so it was, that as oft as he passed*
> *by, he turned in thither to eat bread.*
> *And she said unto her husband, Behold*

now, I perceive that this is an holy man
of God, which passeth by us continually.
Let us make a little chamber, I pray
thee, on the wall; and let us set for him
there a bed, and a table, and a stool,
and a candlestick: and it shall be, when
he cometh to us, that he shall turn in
thither. And it fell on a day, that he
came thither, and he turned into the
chamber, and lay there. And he
[Elisha] *said to Gehazi his servant,*
Call this Shunammite. And when he
had called her, she stood before him
(II Kings 4:8-12).

As the story unfolds, there was a woman in
the town of Shunem who regarded Elisha as a man
of God. Because of her great respect for Elisha,
she offered him room, board, and food whenever
he was in the area. One day Elisha asked Gehazi
to bring the woman to him because he wanted to
know if the woman was in need of anything, and
she told him she was childless. Gehazi then
brought the woman before Elisha and explained
the woman's needs.

When Elisha heard the woman's report, he
prophesied that this time next year she would have
a son. The Shunammite woman thought Elisha was
lying, but sure enough, she got pregnant and gave
birth to a son the following year.

Now Gehazi was present when Elisha prophesied over the woman. He also knew that she did get pregnant and delivered a son. So he saw a real miracle, and maybe that really *charged up* his faith. Yet we see that some time later, Gehazi still evidenced some "heart problems."

The Shunammite woman's child grew up and lived a good, healthy life. One day the child was out in the field, and he suddenly yelled, "My head! My head!" And the boy fell to the ground and within a short time, he died. The mother took her son and layed him on Elisha's bed in Elisha's room and shut the door. She then told her husband that she was going to go and get Elisha and she would be right back. She didn't tell her husband that the boy was dead.

As the woman was approaching, Elisha looked up from his work and saw her in the distance. He said to Gehazi, "Go and see what the Shunammite woman needs." So Gehazi went to the woman and said, "Is everything all right?" And the woman said yes—everything was fine. Then Gehazi asked the woman about her son and her husband. And again, the woman said everything was all right.

I don't know why the woman didn't tell Gehazi that her son had died and that everything was a mess, but I think that her spiritual eyes told her that Gehazi was not the man of faith she needed at the moment. When she came to the top of the hill and saw Elisha, she fell at his feet. And do you know what Gehazi did? He rudely pushed her away. "Get up woman! Don't act like a baby! Come on, and leave Elisha alone!" He was really acting spiritual, wasn't he?

Gehazi was just rude and crude. His heart wasn't prepared to speak godly words to this woman. He wasn't even perceptive enough at this point to realize that all was not well with the woman. But Elisha knew something was going on and he told Gehazi to leave the woman alone. The woman said, "The son God has given me is dead!" Immediately Elisha gave Gehazi his staff and told him to run straight to the city and lay the staff on the boy. But the woman complained. "I don't want this man praying for my son! He has been so nasty to me. I only want you (Elisha) to come!"

We know that Gehazi was probably embarrassed by the woman's words, but he should have watched his words initially:

"The heart of the wise teacheth his mouth, and addeth learning to his lips"
(Proverbs 16:23).

The attitude of Gehazi's heart was not very good, and his words greatly distressed the Shunammite woman. The woman pleaded with Elisha to come instead of Gehazi.

Elisha came to his room where the dead boy lay. He closed the door behind him and laid upon the child. That kid was like meat in a sandwich—he had the anointing from Elisha on the top and the anointing from the mattress, where Elisha slept, on the bottom. After Elisha laid on the boy a second time, the boy awoke from the dead. The boy walked out of the room and there was Gehazi, who probably felt two inches high, because he had really blown his chance to let God give him a miracle of life.

We see that Gehazi had a problem with his heart because his words were not the words of a wise man. You know, there are a lot of Christians with the same problem. They are believing God for a real breakthrough in their finances, but they just keep speaking doubt and unbelief. A person who has built his or her life on the Word of God has a healthy heart. We learn by speaking the truth, and we can bring miracles to our front doors by speaking good things from our hearts.

WHERE IS YOUR TREASURE?

Let's read a little more about Gehazi because this will really help you walk in the supernatural. Earlier we read about Naaman and how he worshipped Nisrock, the pomegranate? Well, one day Gehazi witnessed a great healing in Naaman's life.

Naaman was the captain of the Syrian army. The Bible says that he was a great man and a mighty man of valor. However, Naaman had a serious problem: he was a leper.

One day a servant girl in Naaman's household said:

> . . . *Would God my lord were with the prophet that is in Samaria! for he would recover him of his leprosy* (II Kings 5:3).

Naaman's wife listened to her servant girl and decided to encourage her husband to go and see this prophet. So Naaman went to King Benhadad, and asked him for the day off in order to go and see this prophet. Benhadad said it was okay, and even volunteered to send a letter to the king of Israel. The letter read: "With this letter I am sending my servant Naaman to you so that you may cure him of his leprosy." Naaman then left and took with him gold, silver, and clothing to use as gifts.

The king of Israel got the letter and thought that he was supposed to heal Naaman, and he was very distressed! But Elisha found out, and requested that Naaman come to his house. One day a chariot pulled up in front of Elisha's house, and out stepped Naaman. Naaman had anticipated a fancy greeting, but all he got was a messenger from Elisha. The messenger told Naaman to go to the river Jordan, dip himself seven times in its waters, and he would be healed. Naaman was enraged at this idea; but, eventually, his aides were able to convince him to obey the messenger. We know that Naaman received a marvelous healing that day and our friend Gehazi witnessed it. He saw a leprous man changed instantly by the power of God.

Remember the gifts that Naaman brought with him? After he was healed, Naaman offered to give the gifts to Elisha. But Elisha refused the gifts—because he knew Naaman was trying to "pay" for his miracle. Naaman's miracle was a gift from God that no money could buy, and Elisha wanted Naaman to realize that God was the healer. So Naaman kept the goods and began the return trip home.

However, Gehazi couldn't stop thinking about all the goodies Naaman had stashed away in his chariot. Gehazi thought to himself, "I don't know why Elisha wouldn't take those gifts, but I'm not going to miss this opportunity! It's not everyday that somebody brings gifts of gold and silver! I'm really behind in my chariot payments and I could use the money!"

So Gehazi ran after Naaman and eventually caught up with him. Gehazi lied and said that

Elisha had changed his mind, and could he take the gifts now? Naaman said, "Sure! Go ahead and take all you need!" You can bet that Gehazi wasn't timid. He loaded himself up with the merchandise and quickly went to a secret place to hide his new fortune.

Gehazi thought everything was just fine. He had gotten his treasure from Naaman, and yet Elisha knew nothing of the transaction. He would just continue to be Elisha's servant and privately gloat over his riches.

How many of you know that your sin will find you out! It was clear that Gehazi's heart was full of earthly treasures and not heavenly treasures, and Elisha was not deceived:

> . . . *And Elisha said unto him, Whence comest thou, Gehazi? And he said, Thy servant went no whither. And he [Elisha] said unto him, Went not mine heart with thee, when the man turned again from his chariot to meet thee? Is it a time to receive money, and to receive garments, and oliveyards, and vineyards, and sheep, and oxen, and menservants, and maidservants? The leprosy therefore of Naaman shall cleave unto thee, and unto thy seed for ever. And he went out from his presence a leper as white as snow* (II Kings 5:25-27).

Elisha had discerned Gehazi's sin, "Gehazi, old buddy, I hate to tell you this, but I know you stopped Naaman and took some of his goods. You've lied to me and been disobedient. Since you wanted what Naaman had so badly, you can have his leprosy too!" Instantly Gehazi's skin became diseased with leprosy. The condition of his heart had brought disaster upon him.

Sometimes we Christians try to act "super-spiritual" and pretend that money is just so insignificant. But the fact remains that our treasures usually pertain to money and wealth. Be really honest—isn't it true? Money matters, and God knows that it matters. But God wants your treasure, or your most prized possession, to be a godly heart. Remember, we have said that God wants your heart more than your pocketbook.

Some people place their whole value on how much they are worth in terms of money. They dream about money and talk about money and read about money day and night. Their treasure is in the "what you can see and feel" realm. The Bible says that where your heart is, there also will be your treasure. If your heart is secure in the wisdom of the Word, then that will be your treasure. Because the wisdom of the Word is so good you will begin to grow—and grow. Pretty soon, you will be acting just like the faithful man who believed God for a miracle. Place your treasure with Jesus; He will give you the best return on your investment!

A HEART OF PEACE
GIVES LIFE

Many of you may be thinking, "There is no hope for Gehazi! He is too hard-hearted to receive from God! And now, he has leprosy—yuck!" But how many of you know that God likes to take "terminal heart cases" and do major miracles? Gehazi needed a heart that was ripe for God—a first-fruit heart.

The time of Gehazi's turnaround came near the end of another seven-year famine. This famine had caused many people, including the Shunammite woman and her son, to go and live with the Philistines. However, this action caused the people to give up their homes to the government, and reclaiming them was an almost impossible thing.

Jehoram was the king, and one day he wanted to talk with Gehazi. He wanted to know all the great things that Elisha the prophet had done. Gehazi talked and talked about how Elisha had made the bitter water sweet, how he had healed Naaman, and how he had raised a boy from the dead. Gehazi was full of God and couldn't stop spreading the good news about all the miracles.

As he was talking, who do you suppose walked up but the Shunammite woman:

And it came to pass, as he was telling the king how he [Elisha] *had restored a dead body to life, that, behold, the woman, whose son he had restored to life, cried to the king for her house and for her land. And Gehazi said, My lord, O king, this is the woman, and this is her son, whom Elisha restored to life* (II Kings 8:5).

Here we see a miracle. The woman has just returned from the Philistine camp, yet she knew that she no longer had a house and land. This woman had experienced miracles, so I know she had been praying about her house and her land.

The timing was so perfect. Here came the Shunammite woman, who was believing God for a miracle, and there stood Gehazi. I think he had repented of his sin by then, so God may have given him a new heart. That old hard heart was buried, and Gehazi's new heart was filled with peace, joy and new life:

"A sound heart is the life of the flesh: . . . " (Proverbs 14:30)

The king was so impressed with the message from Gehazi that he turned to the Shunammite woman and said, "Oh, I've been so encouraged by this man that I'm in a giving mood! Here! Take your farm and all your land! It's yours free of charge!'' Gehazi was able to give the Shunammite woman a miracle after all because his heart was full of peace and life. The first fruits of generosity yielded a financial miracle!

We may think that our financial problems are too big even for God. We may not have been faithful in our giving tithes and offerings, and our hearts may be in bad shape. But God is a God of turnarounds, right? If we would repent this moment, God would give us the new heart we so desperately need. With our new heart would come the first fruits of righteousness, and the windows of heaven would pour out miracle blessings just for our need. Isaiah 54:14 says:

> *In righteousness shalt thou be established: thou shalt be far from oppression; for thou shalt not fear: and from terror; for it shall not come near thee.*

Your new heart will allow righteousness to establish you and keep the devil from you. You won't have to fear financial catastrophe, for God is the harvester of your first fruits.

THE ISSUES
OF LIFE

I hope you haven't forgotten our story about

115

Gehazi and the food? At the end of that story, Elisha put the food before the people, and they ate until they were filled. Gehazi missed his chance for a miracle there, but he got back into the miracle flow later.

You have the potential to see first-fruit miracles in your life everyday. The supernatural is at your fingertips, and God is ready to move mountains on your behalf. Maybe you think that it is too late for you. Maybe your heart has been full of unbelief, and you haven't really been faithful in your giving. Well, God loves you anyway. Yes, He loves you even if you have blown it. God wants to give you a new heart so that you can give Him your first fruits. Then God, in return, can give you supernatural miracles for supernatural finances!

Please pray this prayer with me:

"Dear heavenly Father, I know it is Your will that I am prosperous and successful in life. I know You gave me special talents and skills with which to work and earn money, and I thank You. Please forgive me if my heart has worshipped false treasures, and if I have been failing to give of my first fruits. God, right now, I ask You to give me a brand-new heart, one that is clean and pure before You. Fill me with the fruits of righteousness, and establish me in the firm Word of God. Help me to guard my heart, for out of it flows the issues of life. Cleanse me in the blood of Jesus, and give me a freshness in my faith. Make my first fruits bless others as well as myself. Be blessed, Lord, by the sacrifice of my praise to You. In Jesus' name, amen.''

Chapter Six

LOVING YOUR WAY INTO MIRACLES

There are many books on the market today that tell you how to "have it all." You can be rich, handsome, and popular all in one day if you make yourself number one. According to these books, you don't have to stifle your life by being good and moral. Just grab all the "gusto" you can and really live! If your mate is not what you hoped he or she would be, then just get rid of him (or her). Get rid of the things that hurt and the things that make your life less than perfect. Watch out for yourself first though, and when you are "okay," then you can watch out for others.

The system of the world today is very self-centered. "I will make it to the top. I will be good to myself first and my family second. I will not take garbage from anyone else. I will show that guy who is boss around here," and so on. The "me" generation of people are so concerned with themselves and their needs that they can't see the selfish lifestyles they portray. One of the biggest reasons that television isn't good for you is because these selfish and ungodly lifestyles are glorified and exalted. Illicit sex is portrayed without guilt, drunkenness without shame, divorce without remorse, and evil for more evil. These ideas are completely opposite from what the Bible teaches, yet most of the world fails to see the harm in them. If you are always "looking out for number one," then you aren't out looking for God.

"GRUDGES ARE MINE"
SAITH US

Because we are so self-centered and preoccupied with external pleasures, we don't want other people to bother us. When someone causes trouble for us, our first response is to get rid of them. One time a woman asked me why I never taught on worship. I asked her if she was in my services 100 percent of the time last year. She said she hadn't made every one of them. So I said, "Then you *don't know* if I teach on worship or not."

Wasn't that sweet of me? What a kind spirit I demonstrated—so spiritual! This woman had attacked me, and I wanted to get even, right then and there. But the Bible says not to get in strife with people with the intent of getting even because vengeance belongs to God and to God alone.

What exactly is vengeance? The dictionary says *vengeance* is "a punishment inflicted in retaliation for an injury or offense." It's like taking out a grudge on someone with the specific intent to hurt and injure that person. Although you may not physically injure someone during times of vengeance, the fact remains that you still *want to injure* that person. "I'll show him a thing or two for embarrassing me in front of my peers! Just wait until the next time he needs help! I'll nail him to the wall so fast his head will spin. That'll teach him to mess with me!'' Sound familiar? Those are words we use to defend ourselves and to carry out vengeance. We decide to take the matter into our own hands and be the judge, jury, and court-martial. God doesn't want us to be the judge of our own affairs. Instead, God wants to teach us to love our way into miracles.

THE GREAT
COURTROOM OF LIFE

Many of you are familiar with court proceedings. The main thrust of the court system is to prosecute fairly a person accused of a crime. The person is either guilty or not guilty, and sometimes it takes months—or even years—to reach a decision. Well, God has a ''court system'' of His own that has been doing very well for thousands of years. God has a lot of patience, but since He is the Judge, it doesn't take Him years to reach a decision about a matter. God is always fair. He doesn't get confused about right and wrong because He never compromises His Word. Sin is sin. God is very practical about how He runs His courtroom. The world today wants to call sin by another name and compromise God's Word to fit its own needs: ''Well, I know abortion isn't right, but what about the rights of the mother?''

"Living together before marriage may have been wrong a generation ago, but these are the 1990's. We don't need a certificate to prove our love!"

Did you know that excuses for sin can be "conscience killers"? If we paint sin white instead of black, pretty soon our consciences will be deadened to the truth:

> *Unto the pure all things are pure: but unto them that are defiled and unbelieving is nothing pure; but even their mind and conscience is defiled. They profess that they know God; but in works they deny him, being abominable, and disobedient, and unto every good work reprobate* (Titus 1:15-16).

I know you may be thinking, "Marilyn, these are hard words to hear. Can't you tone it down a little?" No, I can't tone it down because that would be a compromise. If God calls something sin, then as Christians we need to do the same thing. We have to do more than profess that we know God; we have to live a life that is obedient to God. We can't be pure when we want to kill our neighbors for accidentally backing into our mailboxes. We can't be holy when we purposely "forget" our mates' birthdays because they forgot our birthdays. We can't live lifestyles that are comfortable for us even though they are uncomfortable for God. Our minds must be renewed to the truth not to the lies of the devil. Seeking vengeance is unholy before God, and our works are defiled.

PROSECUTION ISN'T ALWAYS PRETTY

Let's turn to II Kings 2:23 and look at a situation where people got to messing in God's courtroom, and the prosecution wasn't a pretty sight:

And he [Elisha] *went up from thence unto Bethel: and as he was going up by the way, there came forth little children out of the city, and mocked him, and said unto him, Go up, thou bald head; go up, thou bald head.*

Now this account of the youths mocking Elisha occurred right after the rapture of Elijah. These kids are probably in their late teens or early twenties, and they are making fun of the whole story of Elijah being taken up into heaven—calling him names and then challenging Elisha to go to heaven too. "If you are such a hotshot now, Elisha, go on up to heaven too! Come on! We want to see this with our own eyes! Come on baldy, shoot on up there!" The kids were making fun of the supernatural because they didn't understand the truth.

125

The world makes fun of the supernatural today also. Men of God through whom the Holy Spirit has worked wonderful miracles of healing and even resurrections from the dead have been utterly ridiculed by the news media. Works of the devil such as channeling, mind control, and witchcraft get far less attention. As Christians, we get our feathers ruffled when we are attacked by the world. But, remember, God is the Judge of the whole earth. He knows when the wrong people attack the right people. And believe me, God's judgment is fair and square—it's straight from the Word.

So these kids were calling Elisha crazy and bald. They were mocking Elisha as well as the supernatural rapture of Elijah. Now if Elisha had been operating in the flesh, he might have prayed down fire on them! But Elisha walked in the Spirit, and he wasn't going to seek vengeance. Remember, when we turn matters over to God, He judges the matter, and vengeance belongs to Him alone.

We've learned a great deal about miracles in this book, and we usually think that miracles are good. But God can also bring miracles of judgment that cause people to repent. These kids who mocked Elisha and mocked the rapture and mocked God were ripe for judgment:

And he turned back, and looked on

*them, and cursed them in the name of
the LORD. And there came forth two
she bears out of the wood, and tare
forty and two children of them*
(II Kings 2:24).

Elisha called on the Lord for a miracle of
judgment because of the youths' rebellion and
mockery of the things of God. Notice that Elisha
didn't take the matter into his own hands. He
called on God because vengeance belongs to God.

Do you see why it isn't smart to take things
into your own hands? If Elisha had allowed his
temper to get out of control and had gone after
those boys himself, he would have been in big
trouble. Forty or more boys against one man was
an uneven match. But Elisha did the godly thing.
He gave the matter over to God:

"God, these boys are calling me 'bald head,'
and you know that bothers me. Plus they're
making fun of Elijah and his magnificent exit to
heaven. Please do something here; I give this
matter to You." Taking vengeance into our own
hands is asking for trouble. We need to follow the
rules in God's courtroom in order to win the case.

THE EVIDENCE
OF THE CRIME

When a person has been wronged and

becomes consumed with anger, some sort of retaliation is just around the corner. Yes, it hurts to be hurt. Yes, it is painful to be ridiculed and abused. But God knows the harm in taking vengeance into our own hands. That is why He has given us the Bible as a rule book for living. He loves us enough to tell us the rules of the game before we even bat the ball. The Bible is full of instructions on how to live a godly life. There are rules on finances, sex, child-rearing, relationships with people, and personal godly living. Let's look at God's rules for when we have been wronged:

> *Repay no one evil for evil, but take thought for what is honest and proper and noble* [aiming to be above reproach] *in the sight of everyone. If possible, as far as it depends on you, live at peace with everyone. Beloved, never avenge yourselves, but leave the way open for* [God's] *wrath; for it is written, Vengeance is Mine, I will repay (requite), says the Lord. But, if your enemy is hungry, feed him; if he is thirsty, give him drink; for by so doing you will heap burning coals upon his head. Do not let yourself be overcome by evil, but overcome (master) evil with good* (Romans 12:17-21, TAB).

I know that many of us wish these words were

not in the Bible. Sometimes we would rather say, "Listen, you slug, if you don't stop bothering me, I'm going to paste you to the wall!" That sounds so godly, doesn't it? The Bible says to overcome evil with good, and that is really tough to do. But when we fail to obey the Word, we get into *even worse* messes.

There is a situation in Genesis that turns into a big, big mess because believers took vengeance into their own hands. The story is in Genesis 34 and it deals with the defilement of the daughter of Jacob:

> *And Dinah the daughter of Leah, which she bare unto Jacob, went out to see the daughters of the land. And when Shechem the son of Hamor the Hivite, prince of the country, saw her, he took her, and lay with her, and defiled her* (Genesis 34:1-2).

Dinah was the only daughter of Jacob, and she was very beautiful. She had 11 brothers, and you can bet they kept their eyes on their sister. They weren't going to let "just any man" be seen with her. They were big brothers in every sense of the word.

One day Dinah was taking a walk through the new land into which she had just moved. Shechem, the son of Prince Hamor, was minding his own business until he saw cute little Dinah walking around. He probably thought she was the most gorgeous girl he had ever seen. Lust, not love, filled his heart, and he took Dinah and raped her. Rape is a terrible thing, but, in those days, losing one's virginity before marriage labeled a girl as "defiled." Those who were defiled were treated as social outcasts—with no respect whatsoever.

Now Dinah was no longer a virgin; she had been defiled by Shechem. This was a terrible, terrible situation. But Shechem, despite his horrible deed, loved Dinah. The Bible says he loved her and even asked his father Hamor if he could have Dinah for his wife.

In the meantime, guess who had heard about Dinah's rape? You guessed it—Jacob and all his sons. You can imagine how they felt: Jacob's only daughter and the boys' only sister had been raped and was now "defiled" according to the law. They probably had "kill" flashing from their eyes. The seed of vengeance was firmly planted in their hearts.

If this had happened to *your* daughter, you probably would feel the same way. But since you have had this teaching, you would know that you couldn't take vengeance into your own hands. You would say, "I remember that teaching by Marilyn Hickey that said to love my way into miracles, so that's what I'm going to do. I'm going to love and not hate." God can work a tremendous miracle when the vengeance belongs to Him.

Let's find out what Hamor did about his son's sin. Hamor wanted to make things right with the house of Israel and he wanted a miracle to transpire from all this mess. Hamor didn't try and cover up the crime. He could have said, "Well, Jacob, if your daughter hadn't been flirting with my boy, this wouldn't have happened." No, the evidence clearly showed Shechem as the criminal. All Hamor wanted was a way to reconcile the people back together:

> *And Hamor the father of Shechem went out unto Jacob to commune with him. And the sons of Jacob came out of the field when they heard it: and the men were grieved, and they were very wroth, because he had wrought folly in Israel in lying with Jacob's daughter; which thing ought not to be done. And Hamor communed with them, saying, The soul of my son Shechem longeth for your daughter. I pray you give her him to wife. And make ye marriages with us, and give your daughters unto us, and take our daughters unto you. And ye shall dwell with us: and the land shall be before you; dwell and trade ye therein, and get you possessions therein. And*

> *Shechem said unto her father and unto*
> *her brethren, Let me find grace in your*
> *eyes, . . .* (Genesis 34:6-11).

Hamor and Shechem tried their very best to bring a miracle out of an awful situation. Shechem asked for grace. He even offered to pay whatever Jacob desired if only he would consent to giving Dinah over as his wife. But Jacob's boys had plugged ears. They didn't want good for evil. They wanted vengeance for this terrible crime.

It seems Jacob softened somewhat because he said to Hamor, "Okay, if all of your men will enter into covenant with us and get circumcised like us, then we'll forget this matter and go on." Hamor and Shechem were so eager to clear up the evil act that they agreed to do as Jacob said. So all the Hivite men were brought together and circumcised.

Hamor and Shechem had done all they knew to do to turn the curse into a blessing. But there were two of Dinah's brothers that had vengeance in their hearts:

> *And it came to pass on the third day,*
> *when they* [the men] *were sore, that two*
> *of the sons of Jacob, Simeon and Levi,*
> *Dinah's brethren, took each man his*
> *sword, and came upon the city boldly,*
> *and slew all the males. And they slew*
> *Hamor and Shechem his son with the*

> *edge of the sword, and took Dinah out*
> *of Shechem's house, and went out. The*
> *sons of Jacob came upon the slain, and*
> *spoiled the city, because they had*
> *defiled their sister* (Genesis 34:25-27).

Simeon and Levi, with vengeance in their hearts, killed all the men in the city including Hamor and Shechem. They had all the evidence they needed to warrant the deaths of the criminal and all the other men. All along, Hamor and Shechem had tried to bring healing into the situation. But the sons of Jacob thought that vengeance belonged to them and not to God. Their vengeance did not produce a blessing, but, rather, a curse. When Jacob prophesied over his children, Simeon and Levi got the worst news of all:

> *Simeon and Levi are brethren;*
> *instruments of cruelty are in their*
> *habitations. O my soul, come not thou*
> *into their secret; unto their assembly,*
> *mine honour, be not thou united: for*
> *in their anger they slew a man . . .*
> *Cursed be their anger, for it was fierce;*
> *and their wrath, for it was cruel: I will*
> *divide them in Jacob, and scatter them*
> *in Israel* (Genesis 49:5-7).

Simeon and Levi sowed vengeance; and, because we reap what we sow, we will see how the seeds of vengeance returned to the house of

Israel in a powerful way.

THE JUDGE IS
ON YOUR SIDE

How many of you know that if you sow seeds of *corn*, then you will reap *corn*? If you plant tomatoes, you don't get cantaloupes. You get tomatoes, of course. Whatever kind of seed you sow, that is what you will harvest.

Therefore, if you give out love, what do you think you will get in return? If you said love, you get an A + . If you sow peace, you receive peace. But what if you sow bad seeds like hate and selfishness and strife? What is going to come back on you? That's right, hate, selfishness, and strife will come right back in your lap. If you sow vengeance in a situation, then you've just opened the door for it to come back and visit you. And believe me, that visit won't be pleasant.

Simeon and Levi sowed vengeance into their situation concerning Dinah. They planted seeds of hate all around themselves. Generations later those seeds of vengeance were still multiplying and growing, and we see the result of that harvest of vengeance in Joshua 9:

And when the inhabitants of Gibeon heard what Joshua had done unto Jericho and Ai, They did work wilily,

*and went and made as if they had been
ambassadors, and took old sacks upon
their asses, and wine bottles, old, and
rent, and bound up; And old shoes and
clouted upon their feet, and old
garments upon them; and all the bread
of their provision was dry and moldy.
And they went to Joshua unto the camp
at Gilgal, and said unto him, and to
the men of Israel, We be come from a
far country: now therefore make ye a
league with us* (Joshua 9:3-6).

The men of Gibeon were called Hivites, and
they were descendants of Hamor and Shechem.
Because Israel was such a powerful nation and so
good at wiping out enemy cities, Gibeon wanted
to pursue peace—not war. The threat of war with
Israel meant certain defeat for them. So the men
carefully planned how to trick Israel into coming
into covenant with them—because a covenant
would protect them from war.

The Hivites had devised a plan to deceive
Israel. First, they would pretend they were from
a land far away, because that was an important
condition for signing a covenant with Israel. Since
they were pretending to have travelled a great
distance, the men dressed and acted the part;
"Look here Joshua, you can see my toes hangin'
out of these old shoes! That's how far we've come!

And look here at this bread! It used to be white but now it's green and yucky! And my hair is just a mess! I haven't gone to the barber in months!''

Joshua looked at the men's ragged clothes and moldy bread and was convinced that the men were telling the truth. *Joshua didn't seek God about the matter,* so he fell hook, line, and sinker for the hoax. Joshua said, ''Sure, I'll enter into covenant with you guys; this will be great!''

Little did Joshua know that he had just reaped the seed of vengeance and trickery passed on by Simeon and Levi. Israel had tricked the Hivites, and now the Hivites had just tricked Israel. It was only about three days before Joshua found out that the Gibeonites lived only about 25 miles away in the enemy territory belonging to Canaan. When Joshua discovered the foolish mistake he had made, he was very angry:

> *And Joshua called for them, and he spake unto them, saying, Wherefore have ye beguiled us, saying, We are very far from you; when ye dwell among us? Now therefore ye are cursed, and there shall none of you be freed from being bondmen,* . . .
> (Joshua 9:22-23).

There was nothing Joshua could do now that the Hivites were in covenant with the Israelites. They had to stick up for one another even in battle. But Joshua cursed the Hivites for their actions and announced that they would be slaves to the Israelites. The Hivites had lost their freedom. They were to be wood cutters and water carriers for Israel.

God now has *two* problems to solve. First, Israel reaped the seed of vengeance and was deceived into making a bad covenant. Second, the Hivites, in pursuing peace, lost their freedom. Both parties had made a big mistake. God could have said, ''What am I going to do with you guys? You are always goofing up and making mistakes. I tell you not to take vengeance into your own hands and you do it anyway. Hivites, you acted out the seed of vengeance and Israel, you received it lock, stock, and barrel. This is it guys! I give up on you!''

Do you think that was what God said? No! We know that God always wants the best for His people—even when they blow it! God loves to turn curses into blessings. Even though the natural consequences of sin sometimes must run their course, God can take failure and turn it into success. God is the Judge of the whole world; and, if He is on your side, you've got it made.

There have been so many times that I felt I had really blown it. I had sown strife and vengeance and felt so unspiritual. But God was my Judge, and He was on my side. He wanted to take my mistakes and teach me how to love my way into miracles. You may fall on your face a million times, but God has a million miracles waiting to help you. You may have been sowing vengeance into a particular circumstance for 20 years, but God still wants to free you. Either you can live like the Hatfields and McCoys all your life, or you can let God free you from strife!

Let's see what happened to Joshua and the Hivites. All the other nations were so furious at the Hivites for making a covenant with Israel that they had murder on their minds. They wanted to wipe the Hivites off the earth. And when the Hivites heard this news, they trembled with fear. "Oh, Joshua! We are in *big* trouble here! You've got to help us because you are in covenant with us!" Joshua knew God was on their side, and He would fight the battles for them.

In three different battles, God performed three different miracles to defeat the enemy. One time He confused the enemy so much that they began attacking each other. Another time, God dropped huge balls of hail on the enemy and killed them. And yet another time, God made the sun stand still so there would be enough daylight for Joshua to win the battle. The Israelites and Hivites were in God's courtroom and as long as He was the Head Judge—mercy, forgiveness, grace, and victory would be in full supply.

THE JURY HAS
REACHED A DECISION

You know, one of the things I love about the Bible is that it shows the true nature of people. We all would love to paint a nice, rosy picture about how good and lovely we are. But the only star in this universe is Jesus Christ. He is the only one that hasn't goofed up, and goofed up, and goofed up. He was and is perfect and complete in every way. When our lives fall short of the mark, we turn our eyes to Jesus because He can patch the broken spots and turn a curse into a blessing.

There are many other instances in the Bible where people sought vengeance and got into real trouble. David was one of the most godly men of the Bible, but he often fell short as a father. David had two sons, Amnon and Absalom, and a daughter named Tamar. Now Tamar was the half-sister of Amnon, but the full-blooded sister of Absalom. One day Amnon seduced Tamar and raped her. When Absalom found out, he was simply furious. This sounds familiar, doesn't it? This sounds just like Simeon and Levi and their sister Dinah. Absalom couldn't believe Amnon would do such a thing. He went to his father and even though David was grieved about the situation, he didn't do anything to punish Amnon. And this hurt Absalom. You know, kids need their parents' direction and guidance so they can feel secure and successful. But David wouldn't even touch the matter. So, from that point on, Absalom plotted how to kill Amnon.

Absalom eventually did kill Amnon because that seed of vengeance had been planted. And as that seed of vengeance grew, more and more rebellion and hatred developed in Absalom. The hatred became so vicious that Absalom plotted to take the throne from his father. And in order to take the throne, David would have to be killed. Vengeance, vengeance, vengeance. That's all Absalom thought about. However, the tables turned on Absalom, and later he was the one who died.

Remember Esther, Mordecai, and Haman? Haman was a real hot-head who got all bent out of shape one day because a man named Mordecai wouldn't bow down to him. He got so mad that he decided to kill all the Jews in the land:

> *And when Haman saw that Mordecai bowed not, nor did him reverence, then was Haman full of wrath. And he thought scorn to lay hands on Mordecai alone; for they had shewed him the people of Mordecai: wherefore Haman sought to destroy all the Jews that were throughout the whole kingdom of*

Ahasuerus, even the people of Mordecai (Esther 3:5-6).

Mordecai could have gotten his feathers all ruffled and threatened, ''You'll be sorry you ever messed with me and my people!'' But Mordecai didn't take vengeance. He asked Queen Esther to fast and pray about the situation, and in the end, it was Haman who was hanged on the gallows.

God is not only the best Judge in the world, He has the best jury. He doesn't need a lot of people, because the two He has are the best. God appointed Jesus and the Holy Spirit as the jury to rule in our circumstances. When you fast and pray and let God have the vengeance, you open the door for the miraculous. Mordecai probably wasn't too thrilled about Haman and his childish ways, but he refused to sow vengeance. He gave the vengeance to God, sowed love and prayer, and loved his way into a miracle from God. The Judge and jury overruled defeat for Mordecai. And they can do the same for you.

SENTENCED TO MIRACLE WORKING POWER

When you give God your vengeance, you are ''sentenced'' to a life full of miracles. God says,

"Thank you for the vengeance and don't worry, I'll take care of the offending party for you." Then Jesus and the Holy Spirit get together and plan your miracle, and God the Judge signs the release. There is just no way you can fail when you do things God's way.

One time I heard some terrible gossip about our ministry that had been circling around. At first, I quoted the Word and believed God for a turnaround. But the gossip didn't stop, and one night I woke up *angry*. I said, "God, You said vengeance was Yours, and I haven't seen You take vengeance on anybody that criticized me, not even once. Why don't You take vengeance on anyone that hurts me?" I was really mad at God for not blasting all the people who were spreading the gossip.

God didn't answer me right away. He didn't even say a word to me, which made me feel even more uncomfortable. While I was waiting for God to kill all my enemies, President Reagan was elected to office. It was election night, and the news said that even though Ronald Reagan had had more slander and "garbage" thrown at him than any president in history, he won the election with the greatest number of electoral votes that any president had ever had! Just as I was thinking about that, the Lord spoke to me. "Do you know that I am bigger than 'garbage'?" Suddenly I understood that God will handle the vengeance in His own time. God has had more practice than anyone in handling "garbage" situations, so He doesn't want me to handle "garbage." God can handle the junk and trash of the world so much better than we can, and we need to learn to hand it over to Him.

God wants you to *look, act,* and *feel* like a winner. The Bible says that God always causes us to triumph through Christ Jesus. Christians need to stick with God so they can come out smelling like a rose. We are sentenced to miracles.

There was a man in Poland who presided over all the Pentecostal churches. He was really persecuted by the communists for his faith in God. He lived in an old dumpy, underground apartment with his wife and two kids; and, he pastored a church. This pastor worked so hard that he had a heart attack and had to quit work. Even though the communists were still ugly to him and his family, this man stayed in prayer and believed God for better living conditions for his family. Well, God reached into the heart of a "big wheel" communist who went before the officials and he asked if they would give this pastor an apartment free of charge for the rest of his life. Now, isn't that the hand of God? The pastor didn't get mean or sow vengeance toward the ugly communists. Rather, he gave the problem to God, and God answered with a miracle.

We are sentenced to a life of miracles when we give our grudges to God. We don't have to sow vengeance; we can sow blessings and life. No matter how "impossible" the situation seems, we can love our way into the supernatural power of God. God is the Judge and Jesus and the Holy Spirit are the jury; and when the seed of grace and forgiveness is sown, miracle-working love is grown!

Chapter Seven

WINNING ATTITUDES MAKE MIRACLES

Success in our modern world today is measured in many different ways. If you are a man who subscribes to *Gentleman's Quarterly*, wears Harris-tweed jackets, and owns a Mercedes-Benz, then you are "successful" according to the world's standards. If you are a woman who has a flawless husband and children, attends every school function, and holds down a $50,000 a year job, then you are really something in the world's eyes. Let me tell you, the bigger the gem on your hand, the more admiration you will receive from the world. The more fur you flaunt, the more you'll climb the social ladder. The bigger your house, the greener your lawn, and the more exquisite your country club, the more the world will adore you. People who love wealth and success also love to fill their calendars with big, high-society events so that the world will know that there is a lot of money in their bank accounts.

But do you know that having lots of money, fur coats, and exclusive country club memberships doesn't *really* mean you are successful? Monetarily you may have it all—your gorgeous appearance may put the world's beauties to shame—and your clothes may be prettier and more expensive than Princess Diana's. But you may be missing the *whole key* to lasting success and happiness: a winning attitude.

A lot of research has been done on the lives of millionaires. Studies have shown that most millionaires started out dirt poor. As the years went on, these men and women married and worked out disagreements with their spouses rather than divorce them. Their number-one key to success, outside of the support of their spouses, was an attitude that said, "I won't give up." When the going gets tough, the tough get going. I read a bumper sticker that said, "When the going gets tough, the tough go shopping." I thought that was a great idea, but my husband Wally wasn't too thrilled! Anyway, millionaires share the common thread of thinking and acting successful. They don't allow obstacles to defeat them or hinder them from the desired goal. The word "can't" is not even in their vocabularies.

I know you are thinking, "So what does this have to do with me?" Well, we all need help in our thought life. Having a good attitude can make or break you. Just like a nutritious breakfast is supposed to start your day with a "bang," a winning attitude will make you physically better, intellectually smarter, and spiritually wiser than ever before.

BEATITUDES
FOR ATTITUDES

A winning attitude is essential to gaining and sustaining success. Frequently, we read about people who had lots of money, but committed suicide because they had no hope left. These people had achieved monetary and material success, but they had no success in themselves. Millions of dollars won't make you feel like a winner. Let's face it, we're all going to have some bad times. The world today is rough and tough, and it doesn't pat you on the back very often. Money can be hard to earn, jobs may be hard to keep, marriages may be rocking and rolling every which way, children may be rebellious, and mates may drink and take drugs. These are hard times in this life, and many of us already know that very well. But a winning attitude can be the difference. It could make the difference between one person who has lost everything and starts over again, and another person who has also lost everything but commits suicide.

When you feel like you're living in the pits, how do you go about developing a winning attitude? How can you smile and believe God for a miracle when your husband is mad at you, your kids won't obey you, and the dog just dug up your garden? Do you go out and buy self-help books written by worldly people? Do you join a meditation class, dabble in the occult, and invite the devil to help you? No, a thousand times, no! When you're in troubled waters, don't ask for a tidal wave! Get in tune with God, and ask Him to make those troubled waters into rivers of life! The Bible is full of good counsel and advice on how to get from "the pits to the penthouse." One of the best places in the Word to start remodeling your attitude is in Matthew 5. What you need are some beatitudes for your attitudes!

STAMPING OUT DISCOURAGEMENT

The force of discouragement is very devastating. It can rob you of all hope and strength. Did you know that discouragement is the opposite of courage? Let's pause for a brief English lesson. The prefix "dis" sometimes indicates "not" or "the opposite of." Therefore, the "dis" in front of a word tells us that it is opposite from the root word. For example, *to disobey* means "not to obey." *Discontent* is the opposite of being content. So, when you are *discouraged,* you are actually walking around without any courage!

One of the discouraging things about bad circumstances is that they can make you feel very weak and disabled. In the natural, things may be so awful that you've lost hope, and despair robs you of your strength. Some people have told me that they just plain feel empty—like there is nothing left inside with which to fight.

When problems come, one of the first battle-fields is the mind. The devil loves to throw "brain teasers" at us which are contrary to the Word: "You are a big, fat zero and will never amount to anything," or "Why try to get out of this mess? You won't make it anyway. You might as well just give up!" The arena of the mind is where most battles are either won or lost.

I love the way the dictionary defines *courage:* "An ingrained capacity for meeting strain or stress with fortitude and resilience." God has given us the mental edge to overcome adversity with His help. We don't have to fall victim to the "blues" when we walk by God's rules.

Let's read Matthew 5:6:

"Blessed are they which do hunger and thirst after righteousness: for they shall be filled."

The Amplified Bible says *to be blessed* is to be "fortunate and happy and spiritually prosperous." That's good news! When people go after God, God goes after them! You don't have to run around with an empty gas tank in your car when gas stations are so accessible. It's the same way with Christians. You don't have to run around discouraged and empty when you can be filled and satisfied by seeking after the things of God.

In II Kings 4:38-41 we read about a very discouraging situation. Elisha was the prophet; and, at this particular time, there was a famine in the land. People were tired, hungry, and generally in despair over the circumstances.

Elisha had made a trip to Gilgal to meet with the sons of other prophets. After visiting for quite awhile, the men began to get hungry. So one of the prophets got up and went to the fields to see if he could find something growing wild to eat. Remember, there was a famine in the land, and food was scarce. Let's read what happened:

> *And one went out into the field to gather herbs, and found a wild vine, and gathered thereof wild gourds his lap full, and came and shred them into the pot of pottage: for they knew them not. So they poured out for the men to eat. And it came to pass, as they were eating of the pottage, that they cried out, and said, O thou man of God, there is death in the pot. And they could not eat thereof* (II Kings 4:39-40).

The men had eaten of the unknown gourds and almost immediately they began to feel sick. They cried out with pain and said, "Hey, Elisha, this stuff is poisonous! You are a man of God, help us!'' Since idolatry was so pronounced in the land, you would have thought that someone would have called, ''Baal, Baal! Come quickly and help us!'' But the men sought after the God of Elisha.

What Elisha did was very interesting. He knew the men were reaching out to God. They were, in essence, hungering and thirsting after righteousness. When you are down and out, sometimes you cry to God because you know His ways work. Elisha took some meal and poured it into the stew, and the stew was no longer poisonous. Just like Elisha had poured salt into the bitter waters and healed the water, the meal healed the stew. Now it wasn't actually ''healing meal'' or anything like that. The meal was simply the means God had Elisha use to heal the food. It was a symbol just like the salt in the water was a symbol.

When you hunger and thirst after God, your attitude is going to change. Discouragement can *poison* your faith, but righteousness can *heal* your faith. What had caused death in your situation before, will now be changed to life. A lot of people are afraid to seek after God because they don't think anything new will happen. But the Bible says you will be blessed, that is, happy and fortunate and fully satisfied by going after spiritual ways. Getting out of the blues will bring the miracle of good news!

PURE IN HEART

There are those of us who have had poison in our past. There may have been abuse, incest, strife, adultery, divorce, or death that has hurt us and made us feel sick.

For every bad thing that has ever happened to you, God has a good thing. He has an antidote for poison that will take away your sickness from you:

"Blessed are the pure in heart: for they shall see God" (Matthew 5:8).

When your attitude has been polluted by the poison of the past, you can't see God too well. One of the Greek definitions of *pure* is "to be clean or clear." If your past is muddied with junk and trash, then the way is unsure and wobbly at times. If you feel dirty because of sin, then there may be times when you don't feel very good about yourself. It's hard to feel like a winner when the devil keeps taunting that you are a loser.

God wants to heal the poison of your past. He wants to put His life into you and take away all the pain, and misery, and discouragement. As you purpose in your heart to walk pure before the Lord, you will see glimpses of that winning attitude coming into focus. Success will become a reality for perhaps the first time in your life. When the devil comes at you and tells you that you won't make it, tell him to shut up. And say it like you mean it. You're not a wimp, you're a child of the living God. Like the sign that says, "Just Say No To Drugs," you can just say "No" to the devil. Then that arena in your head no longer can be used by the devil. Make up your mind right now to win and watch the miracles come and come and come!

ARE YOU A PEACEMAKER?

Did you know that your old nature is ugly? That's right, ugly. Your flesh wants to be unspiritual all the time—and that can be a real problem. Your spirit man wants to act like God and your flesh wants to act like the devil, therefore creating a real problem in developing a winning attitude.

You know that I am a pastor's wife; and believe me, after more than 30 years in the ministry, I have seen it all. People get offended over the silliest things; sometimes I want to tell them to "knock it off"! My flesh gets bent out of shape, and I just want to fight, fight, fight! But I *don't* want to act like the devil. He's not my father, and I don't want to imitate his actions because they aren't spiritual at all. So, when my flesh starts acting rude and crude, I know I better get ready for spiritual warfare and stand firm on the Word. I may have to quote the same Bible verse for days or even months until the battle is over. But let me tell you, I'm sticking with God; and He will put me over. He'll keep working on me until my spirit man is strong and my attitudes are right. God is in the whole-man-remodeling business and no job is too big for Him.

ENEMY TERRITORY

In II Kings we have a situation in which a certain king had a very ugly attitude:

> *Then the king of Syria warred against Israel, and took counsel with his servants, saying, In such and such a place shall be my camp. And the man of God sent unto the king of Israel, saying, Beware that thou pass not such a place; for thither the Syrians are come down. And the king of Israel sent to the place which the man of God told him and warned him of, and saved himself there, not once nor twice. Therefore the heart of the king of Syria was sore troubled for this thing; and he called his servants, and said unto*

them, Will ye not shew me which of us
is for the king of Israel? And one of his
servants said, None, my lord, O king:
but Elisha, the prophet that is in Israel,
telleth the king of Israel the words that
thou speakest in thy bedchamber
(II Kings 6:8-12).

Now we know the name of the king of Syria because we have studied him already. Remember? The king's name was Benhadad, and the captain of his army was Naaman. Benhadad had no doubt heard of Naaman's miraculous healing from leprosy, but that wasn't enough to convince him to turn his life over to God. Benhadad continued to rebel against God and Israel. The problem was that Benhadad wanted to capture Israel; and no matter how well he planned his surprise attacks, he couldn't succeed with his plans. For some strange reason, Israel knew Benhadad's every move before he even made it. Benhadad got so upset he accused his own men of tipping off the enemy beforehand. But one of the men stood up and said, "Hey, it's not us, it's Elisha! His God tells him everything about us!"

With his lightening quick mind, Benhadad figured out that the only way to stop God from talking to Elisha was to capture him and put him in jail. You see, the devil thinks that if he can get you into a bad situation, then God will forget where you are and what you're doing. The devil will get you into strife with your neighbor—and sometimes it gets so bad that your neighbor becomes a full-fledged enemy. But did you know that even when you have an enemy God wants to make you into a peacemaker? He hasn't forgotten you and your situation. God has a beatitude for your attitude:

> *"Blessed are the peacemakers: for they shall be called the children of God"* (Matthew 5:9).

The Amplified Bible says that peacemakers are "makers and maintainers of peace." People who are continually fighting with others have a loser's attitude. They argue and bicker with their families, their employers, their fellow workers, and anyone else who happens to cross their path. Success is hard to come by in these people because they don't have that ingrained capacity to stand up against stress and strain.

It's a hard thing to have a winning attitude when you're surrounded by enemies. Yet God tells us to be makers of peace. Isn't it true that we are supposed to be "fishers of men" when it comes to saving souls? Well, God also wants us to be "makers of peace" with our enemies. The Word says that if we will focus our attitudes on peace, then we will be called the children of God—the children of God have a rich, rich inheritance!

Benhadad was not a peacemaker, he was a troublemaker. He had a bad attitude, and if you noticed, he wasn't very successful. If you were called to be a warrior, then you would hope to be a good one, right? Old Benhadad couldn't even find the army he was supposed to raid! With failure after failure to his credit, the king decided to come up with Plan B and capture Elisha. But God intervened with a tremendous miracle.

PERSECUTED FOR THE WORD'S SAKE

Now we know that Benhadad wasn't too swift because he never caught on to the supernatural workings of God all around him. He was so carnal and fleshly in his thinking that he was blinded by his darkness. If you knew that God was on Elisha's side, would you try and capture him? No, because you know you can't mess with God's property and get away with it. God is always for His people!

But Benhadad was full of rebellion and he devised a plan to take Elisha captive:

And he said, Go and spy where he is, that I may send and fetch him. And it was told him, saying, Behold, he is in Dothan. Therefore sent he thither horses, and chariots, and a great host: and they came by night, and compassed the city about (II Kings 6:13-14).

Benhadad completely surrounded Dothan with multitudes of horses and chariots. He was going to get Elisha if it was the last thing he did! Yet there was one small problem Benhadad did not foresee: God was on Elisha's team, and God has never lost a game! If God is on your side, then you can know for sure that you will never lose either.

FEAR CAN CAPTURE OUR FAITH

When persecutions come—and we know they do—fear can become a dominant force. When you really start to do things for God, get prepared for persecutions and trials. You may think you are the nicest person in the whole world. But I have news for you—the devil doesn't think you're so nice and he wants you to suffer a lot. Satan wants to harass you and injure you and cause you pain simply because he hates what God loves. Some people believe that God sends persecutions to make us better people. If that's the case, load on the troubles—because we all want to be better! But the Bible says that even while we were still in our sins, Jesus died on the Cross for us. Jesus didn't wait until we were sweet and wonderful to die for us. He laid down His life so that someday we could wear crowns! Persecutions are bad times with a special delivery notice from the devil—*but you don't have to sign for the package.*

When you believe the devil's lies, you are soon going to have a "faith attack." In other words, your faith is going to be injured. Heart attacks are caused by heart failure. "Faith attacks" are caused by Word failure. If you let the disease of the devil choke out the Word of God, then your faith for the miraculous dies. When fear fills the place of faith, you get weaker and weaker and weaker.

But persecutions *don't have to rob us* of our faith:

> *"Blessed are they which are persecuted for righteousness' sake: for their's is the kingdom of heaven"* (Matthew 5:10).

The enemy can be all around us, yet our knees don't have to buckle with fear. God is with us! When you are in enemy territory, and you've been walking upright before the Lord, the Bible says the kingdom of heaven is at hand. All of the forces of heaven are with you during your times of trial, so rejoice! God says you are blessed and prosperous no matter how horrible the situation seems! God has a thousand ways to reveal His strength and power to you; and, one way may be to open your eyes to the supernatural.

161

SUPERNATURAL SIGHTS

Benhadad had set up his forces during the night when all the people of Dothan were asleep. When the servant of Elisha got up the next morning, he was horrified to see the city totally surrounded by the Syrian army:

> *And when the servant of the man of God was risen early, and gone forth, behold, an host compassed the city both with horses and chariots. And his servant said unto him, Alas, my master! how shall we do?* (II Kings 6:15).

There are a lot of Christians just like this servant boy. We see bad circumstances and yell, "What shall we do? Help! We need help!" We run to God, but if He doesn't answer us fast enough, then our winning attitudes turn into sinning attitudes: "Oh, why do I bother anyway? I'm just a big flop! My mother was a flop, my brother was a flop, and I'm a flop. I'm just going to give up!" Our faith turns to fear, and we can't see beyond the enemy's lines. But God can see farther than we can. He knows that persecutions are only temporary; and if we'll look for the supernatural and believe that we will win, then miracles are going to happen.

Elisha turned to the young servant boy
and said:

> . . . *Fear not: for they that be with us*
> *are more than they that be with them.*
> *And Elisha prayed, and said, LORD,*
> *I pray thee, open his eyes, that he may*
> *see. And the LORD opened the eyes of*
> *the young man; and he saw: and,*
> *behold, the mountain was full of horses*
> *and chariots of fire round about Elisha*
> (II Kings 6:16-17).

When you get in line with God and focus your
attitudes on miracles, you, too, will see the armies
of God surrounding your situation. Sometimes
people may be your enemies. Sometimes money
may be your enemy. Sometimes your children may
be the biggest enemies you have because they are
so rebellious. But if you keep your eyes on God,
you will win. Why? Because you are blessed for
being upright and godly, and you will not be
forsaken in your time of need.

REJOICE AND BE
EXCEEDINGLY GLAD

Benhadad had a plan to capture Elisha and,
eventually, to capture Israel also. The devil may
have plans to capture you—or your family—or
your kids—or your job. He may surround you with

every kind of enemy artillery he can find. But the Bible says to rejoice and be glad:

> *Blessed (happy, to be envied, and spiritually prosperous—with life-joy and satisfaction in God's favor and salvation, regardless of your outward conditions) are you when people revile you and persecute you and say all kinds of evil things against you falsely on My account. Be glad and supremely joyful, for your reward in heaven is great (strong and intense), . . .* (Matthew 5:11-12, TAB).

God says that when the enemy in your life comes to tell you that you are a loser, be joyful! Anybody who does anything for God will get some mud slung at them. Anybody who lives a godly life and puts evil away will be the laugh of the party. But God never said that being a Christian would be a "cakewalk." It's a lot of hard work, but the rewards are well worth it all. God will grant you success if you set your attitudes on beatitudes. Don't mope around the house and lose your winning attitude just because somebody calls you names. Jesus was called all kinds of things, but He kept his eyes on the goal and died for the name-callers as well as for the righteous. Jesus never gave up—and neither should you.

SET THE
ENEMY FREE

Let's read what happened to the army of Syria:

And when they came down to him, Elisha prayed unto the LORD, and said, Smite this people, I pray thee, with blindness. And he smote them with blindness according to the word of Elisha. And Elisha said unto them, This is not the way, neither is this the city: follow me, and I will bring you to the man whom ye seek. But he led them to Samaria. And it came to pass, when they were come into Samaria, that Elisha said, LORD, open the eyes of these men, that they may see. And the LORD opened their eyes, and they saw; and, behold, they were in the midst of Samaria (II Kings 6:18-20).

Elisha was a man of God. He didn't pray that God would kill the enemy. He had a mercy motive, remember? Rather, he asked God to temporarily blind the men so that he could lead them to the king of Israel. Did Elisha want Jehoram, the king of Israel, to kill them? No, he had another plan:

And he [Elisha] *answered, Thou shalt not smite them: wouldest thou smite those whom thou hast taken captive with thy sword and with thy bow? set bread and water before them, and they may eat and drink, and go to their master. And he* [Jehoram] *prepared great provision for them: and when they had eaten and drunk, he sent them away, and they went to their master. So the bands of Syria came no more into the land of Israel* (II Kings 6:22,23).

You know, the devil wants to give us an attitude problem. He wants us to seek vengeance on our enemies. He wants us to get into all kinds of vicious revenge in order to keep us from becoming all that God wants us to be. God wants us to free the enemies in our lives by praying love and mercy for them. He wants us to let Jesus handle the battle so that we can stay free from trouble. Elisha knew that killing all those men wasn't the answer. By showing mercy, Israel would reap mercy.

All those men, who probably were scared silly that this was the appointed day to die, sat down to a wonderful meal prepared by the very nation they had sought to destroy. And when they were finished eating, Elisha said, "Okay, boys, dinner is over. It's getting late, so why don't you run along, and we hope never to see you again.''

The army of Syria didn't have to think twice about Elisha's words. They ran home to Benhadad and explained the whole thing: ''You won't believe this, but all of a sudden we went blind and this guy, who turned out to be Elisha, led us to Jehoram and instead of killing us they fed us dinner. Then Elisha told us to go home and never come back again!'' As old Benhadad listened to this news, he knew he had experienced the supernatural.

I have had some attitude problems in my life. ''So-and-so didn't treat me right,'' I would complain. But one day the Lord said that I would never change people with that kind of attitude. I was acting out of my old attitude and griping about persecutions instead of rejoicing. I held my enemies captive instead of freeing them to God. And until I repented of my actions, I didn't see many miracles in those circumstances.

God wants you to be a winner. He wants you to hook into those beatitudes that will change your attitudes. You don't have to have ''faith attacks.'' You don't have to be surrounded by failure and defeat. The devil is *not* your father, and you don't have to live in the pit when you can live in the penthouse! You can rise above the poisons and the enemies in your life with an attitude that is steadfast, not bedfast! Never forget that you are destined for success and that God is behind you all the way.

Chapter Eight

MIRACLE SCRIPTURES

SPIRIT

"Thy word have I hid in mine heart, that I might not sin against thee. Blessed art thou, O LORD: teach me thy statutes" (Psalms 119:11,12).

"Are they not all ministering spirits, sent forth to minister for them who shall be heirs of salvation?" (Hebrews 1:14).

No weapon that is formed against thee shall prosper; and every tongue that shall rise against thee in judgment thou shalt condemn. This is the heritage of the servants of the LORD, and their righteousness is of me, saith the LORD (Isaiah 54:17).

So shall they fear the name of the LORD from the west, and his glory from the rising of the sun. When the enemy shall come in like a flood, the Spirit of the LORD shall lift up a standard against him (Isaiah 59:19).

Verily I say unto you, Whatsoever ye shall bind on earth shall be bound in heaven: and whatsoever ye shall loose on earth shall be loosed in heaven (Matthew 18:18).

Again I say unto you, That if two of you shall agree on earth as touching any thing that they shall ask, it shall be done for them of my Father which is in heaven (Matthew 18:19).

"Therefore I say unto you, What things soever ye desire, when ye pray, believe that ye receive them, and ye shall have them" (Mark 11:24).

Behold, I give unto you power to tread on serpents and scorpions, and over all the power of the enemy: and nothing shall by any means hurt you (Luke 10:19).

"Fear not, little flock; for it is your Father's good pleasure to give you the kingdom" (Luke 12:32).

"But as many as received him, to them gave he power to become the sons of God, even to them that believe on his name" (John 1:12).

For the Father loveth the Son, and sheweth him all things that himself doeth: and he will shew him greater works than these, that ye may marvel (John 5:20).

Peace I leave with you, my peace I give unto you: not as the world giveth, give I unto you. Let not your heart be troubled, neither let it be afraid (John 14:27).

"And the peace of God, which passeth all understanding, shall keep your hearts and minds through Christ Jesus" (Philippians 4:7).

"Hitherto have ye asked nothing in my name: ask, and ye shall receive, that your joy may be full" (John 16:24).

"Nay, in all these things we are more than conquerors through him that loved us" (Romans 8:37).

Now thanks be unto God, which always causeth us to triumph in Christ, and maketh manifest the savour of his knowledge by us in every place (II Corinthians 2:14).

For though we walk in the flesh, we do not war after the flesh: (For the weapons of our warfare are not carnal, but mighty through God to the pulling down of strong holds;) Casting down imaginations, and every high thing that exalteth itself against the knowledge of God, and bringing into captivity every thought to the obedience of Christ (II Corinthians 10:3-5).

I am crucified with Christ: nevertheless I live; yet not I, but Christ liveth in me: and the life which I now live in the flesh I live by the faith of the Son of God, who loved me, and gave himself for me (Galatians 2:20).

Wherefore take unto you the whole armour of God, that ye may be able to withstand in the evil day, and having done all, to stand. Stand therefore, having your loins girt about with truth, and having on the breastplate of righteousness; And your feet shod with the preparation of the gospel of peace; Above all, taking the shield of faith, wherewith ye shall be able to quench all the fiery darts of the wicked. And take the helmet of salvation, and the sword of the Spirit, which is the word of God: Praying always with all prayer and supplication in the Spirit, and watching thereunto with all perseverance and supplication for all saints (Ephesians 6:13-18).

"For it is God which worketh in you both to will and to do of his good pleasure" (Philippians 2:13).

And this is the confidence that we have in him, that, if we ask any thing according to his will, he heareth us: And if we know that he hear us, whatsoever we ask, we know that we have the petitions that we desired of him (I John 5:14,15).

And he shall turn the heart of the fathers to the children, and the heart of the children to their fathers, lest I come and smite the earth with a curse (Malachi 4:6).

And, having made peace through the blood of his cross, by him to reconcile all things unto himself; by him, I say, whether they be things in earth, or things in heaven (Colossians 1:20).

BODY

And said, If thou wilt diligently hearken to the voice of the LORD thy God, and wilt do that which is right in his sight, and wilt give ear to his commandments, and keep all his statutes, I will put none of these diseases upon thee, which I have brought upon the Egyptians: for I am the LORD that healeth thee (Exodus 15:26).

"Thou shalt be blessed above all people: there shall not be male or female barren among you, or among your cattle" (Deuteronomy 7:14).

"O LORD my God, I cried unto thee, and thou hast healed me" (Psalms 30:2).

175

Why art thou cast down, O my soul? and why art thou disquieted within me? hope thou in God: for I shall yet praise him, who is the health of my countenance, and my God (Psalm 42:11).

"My flesh and my heart faileth: but God is the strength of my heart, and my portion for ever" (Psalms 73:26).

"Who forgiveth all thine iniquities; who healeth all thy diseases" (Psalms 103:3).

"The LORD shall preserve thy going out and thy coming in from this time forth, and even for evermore" (Psalms 121:8).

"Be not wise in thine own eyes: fear the LORD, and depart from evil. It shall be health to thy navel, and marrow to thy bones" (Proverbs 3:7,8).

My son, attend to my words; incline thine ear unto my sayings. Let them not depart from thine eyes; keep them in the midst of thine heart. For they are life unto those that find them, and health to all their flesh (Proverbs 4:20-22).

He giveth power to the faint; and to them that have no might he increaseth strength. Even the youths shall faint and be weary, and the young men shall utterly fall: But they that wait upon the LORD shall renew their strength; they shall mount up with wings as eagles; they shall run, and not be weary; and they shall walk, and not faint (Isaiah 40:29-31).

Surely he hath borne our griefs, and carried our sorrows: yet we did esteem him stricken, smitten of God, and afflicted. But he was wounded for our transgressions, he was bruised for our iniquities: the chastisement of our peace was upon him; and with his stripes we are healed (Isaiah 53:4,5).

That it might be fulfilled which was spoken by Esaias the prophet, saying, Himself took our infirmities, and bare our sicknesses (Matthew 8:17).

Who his own self bare our sins in his own body on the tree, that we, being dead to sins, should live unto righteousness: by whose stripes ye were healed (I Peter 2:24).

And the LORD shall guide thee continually, and satisfy thy soul in drought, and make fat thy bones: and thou shalt be like a watered garden, and like a spring of water, whose waters fail not (Isaiah 58:11).

"Heal the sick, cleanse the lepers, raise the dead, cast out devils: freely ye have received, freely give" (Matthew 10:8).

And these signs shall follow them that believe; In my name shall they cast out devils; they shall speak with new tongues; They shall take up serpents; and if they drink any deadly thing, it shall not hurt them; they shall lay hands on the sick, and they shall recover (Mark 16:17,18).

The thief cometh not, but for to steal, and to kill, and to destroy: I am come that they might have life, and that they might have it more abundantly (John 10:10).

And be not conformed to this world: but be ye transformed by the renewing of your mind, that ye may prove what is that good, and acceptable, and perfect, will of God (Romans 12:2).

"For who hath known the mind of the Lord, that he may instruct him? But we have the mind of Christ" (I Corinthians 2:16).

"For God hath not given us the spirit of fear; but of power, and of love, and of a sound mind" (II Timothy 1:7).

Christ hath redeemed us from the curse of the law, being made a curse for us: for it is written, Cursed is every one that hangeth on a tree (Galatians 3:13).

"I can do all things through Christ which strengtheneth me" (Philippians 4:13).

"But my God shall supply all your need according to his riches in glory by Christ Jesus" (Philippians 4:19).

"Beloved, I wish above all things that thou mayest prosper and be in health, even as thy soul prospereth" (III John 2).

ELEMENTS

Then spake Joshua to the LORD in the day when the LORD delivered up the Amorites before the children of Israel, and he said in the sight of Israel, Sun, stand thou still upon Gibeon; and thou, Moon, in the valley of Ajalon. And the sun stood still, and the moon stayed, until the people had avenged themselves upon their enemies. Is not this written in the book of Jasher? So the sun stood still in the midst of heaven, and hasted not to go down about a whole day (Joshua 10:12,13).

And Elijah the Tishbite, who was of the inhabitants of Gilead, said unto Ahab, As the LORD God of Israel liveth, before whom I stand, there shall not be dew nor rain these years, but according to my word (I Kings 17:1).

"And it shall be, that thou shalt drink of the brook; and I have commanded the ravens to feed thee there" (I Kings 17:4).

For thus saith the LORD God of Israel, The barrel of meal shall not waste, neither shall the cruse of oil fail, until the day that the LORD sendeth rain upon the earth. And the barrel of meal wasted not, neither did the cruse of oil fail, according to the word of the LORD, which he spake by Elijah (I Kings 17:14,16).

Hear me, O LORD, hear me, that this people may know that thou art the LORD God, and that thou hast turned their heart back again. Then the fire of the LORD fell, and consumed the burnt sacrifice, and the wood, and the stones, and the dust, and licked up the water that was in the trench (I Kings 18:37,38).

And Isaiah the prophet cried unto the LORD: and he brought the shadow ten degrees backward, by which it had gone down in the dial of Ahaz (II Kings 20:11).

Behold, I will bring again the shadow of the degrees, which is gone down in the sun dial of Ahaz, ten degrees backward. So the sun returned ten degrees, by which degrees it was gone down (Isaiah 38:8).

"Let not the waterflood overflow me, neither let the deep swallow me up, and let not the pit shut her mouth upon me" (Psalms 69:15).

"Tremble, thou earth, at the presence of the Lord, at the presence of the God of Jacob" (Psalms 114:7).

"With my lips have I declared all the judgments of thy mouth" (Psalms 119:13)

They shall take up serpents; and if they drink any deadly thing, it shall not hurt them; they shall lay hands on the sick, and they shall recover (Mark 16:18).

When thou passest through the waters, I will be with thee; and through the rivers, they shall not overflow thee: when thou walkest through the fire, thou shalt not be burned; neither shall the flame kindle upon thee (Isaiah 43:2).

They shall not hunger nor thirst; neither shall

the heat nor sun smite them: for he that hath mercy on them shall lead them, even by the springs of water shall he guide them (Isaiah 49:10).

And the princes, governors, and captains, and the king's counsellors, being gathered together, saw these men, upon whose bodies the fire had no power, nor was an hair of their head singed, neither were their coats changed, nor the smell of fire had passed on them (Daniel 3:27).

Quenched the violence of fire, escaped the edge of the sword, out of weakness were made strong, waxed valiant in fight, turned to flight the armies of the aliens (Hebrews 11:34).

My God hath sent his angel, and hath shut the lions' mouths, that they have not hurt me: forasmuch as before him innocency was found in me; and also before thee, O king, have I done no hurt (Daniel 6:22).

"Who through faith subdued kingdoms, wrought righteousness, obtained promises, stopped the mouths of lions" (Hebrews 11:33).

Yea, the LORD will answer and say unto his people, Behold, I will send you corn, and wine, and oil, and ye shall be satisfied therewith: and

I will no more make you a reproach among the heathen. And the floors shall be full of wheat, and the vats shall overflow with wine and oil. And I will restore to you the years that the locust hath eaten, the cankerworm, and the caterpiller, and the palmerworm, my great army which I sent among you. And ye shall eat in plenty, and be satisfied, and praise the name of the LORD your God, that hath dealt wondrously with you: and my people shall never be ashamed (Joel 2:19, 24-26).

Be glad then, ye children of Zion, and rejoice in the LORD your God: for he hath given you the former rain moderately, and he will cause to come down for you the rain, the former rain, and the latter rain in the first month (Joel 2:23).

"And he said, Come. And when Peter was come down out of the ship, he walked on the water, to go to Jesus" (Matthew 14:29).

"And he arose, and rebuked the wind, and said unto the sea, Peace, be still. And the wind ceased, and there was a great calm" (Mark 4:39).

For verily I say unto you, That whosoever shall say unto this mountain, Be thou removed, and be thou cast into the sea; and shall not doubt in his heart, but shall believe that those things

183

which he saith shall come to pass; he shall have whatsoever he saith (Mark 11:23).

And Jesus took the loaves; and when he had given thanks, he distributed to the disciples, and the disciples to them that were set down; and likewise of the fishes as much as they would. When they were filled, he said unto his disciples, Gather up the fragments that remain, that nothing be lost (John 6:11,12).

And he said unto them, Cast the net on the right side of the ship, and ye shall find. They cast therefore, and now they were not able to draw it for the multitude of fishes (John 21:6).

And when they were come up out of the water, the Spirit of the Lord caught away Philip, that the eunuch saw him no more: and he went on his way rejoicing (Acts 8:39).

Receive Jesus Christ as Lord and Savior of Your Life.

The Bible says, *"That if thou shalt confess with thy mouth the Lord Jesus, and shalt believe in thine heart that God hath raised him from the dead, thou shalt be saved. For with the heart man believeth unto righteousness; and with the mouth confession is made unto salvation"* (Romans 10:9,10).

To receive Jesus Christ as Lord and Savior of your life, sincerely pray this prayer from your heart:

Dear Jesus,

I believe that You died for me and that You rose again on the third day. I confess to You that I am a sinner and that I need Your love and forgiveness. Come into my life, forgive my sins, and give me eternal life. I confess You now as my Lord. Thank You for my salvation!

Signed _____

Date _____

Write to us.
We will send you information to help you with your new life in Christ.

Marilyn Hickey Ministries • P.O. Box 17340
Denver, CO 80217 • (303) 770-0400

For Your Information
Free Monthly Magazine

☐ Please send me your free monthly magazine
  OUTPOURING (including daily devotionals,
  timely articles, and ministry updates)!

Tapes and Books

☐ Please send me Marilyn's latest product catalog.

Mr. & Mrs.   Please print.
Miss
Mrs.
Name Mr. _____

Address _____

City_____

State _____ Zip_____

Phone (H) (   ) _____

     (W) (   ) _____

Mail to
Marilyn Hickey Ministries
P.O. Box 17340
Denver, CO 80217
(303) 770-0400

BOOKS BY MARILYN HICKEY

A Cry for Miracles ($5.95)
Acts of the Holy Spirit ($7.95)
Angels All Around ($7.95)
Armageddon ($3.95)
Ask Marilyn ($8.95)
Be Healed ($8.95)
The Bible Can Change You ($12.95)
The Book of Revelation Comic Book ($3.00)
Break the Generation Curse ($7.95)
Daily Devotional ($5.95)
Dear Marilyn ($5.95)
Divorce Is Not the Answer ($4.95)
Especially for Today's Woman ($14.95)
Freedom From Bondages ($4.95)
Gift Wrapped Fruit ($2.00)
God's Covenant for Your Family ($5.95)
God's Rx for a Hurting Heart ($3.50)
How To Be a Mature Christian ($5.95)
Know Your Ministry ($3.50)
Maximize Your Day . . . God's Way ($7.95)
Release the Power of the Blood Covenant ($3.95)
The Names of God ($7.95)
The No. 1 Key to Success—Meditation ($3.50)
Satan-Proof Your Home ($7.95)
Save the Family Promise Book ($14.95)
Signs in the Heavens ($5.95)
What Every Person Wants to Know About Prayer ($3.95)
When Only a Miracle Will Do ($3.95)
Your Miracle Source ($3.50)
Your Personality Workout ($5.95)
Your Total Health Handbook—Body • Soul • Spirit ($9.95)

MINI-BOOKS: 75¢ each
by Marilyn Hickey

Beat Tension
Bold Men Win
Bulldog Faith
Change Your Life
Children Who Hit the Mark
Conquering Setbacks
Experience Long Life
Fasting and Prayer
God's Benefit: Healing
God's Seven Keys to Make You Rich
Hold On to Your Dream
How To Become More Than a Conqueror
How To Win Friends
I Can Be Born Again and Spirit Filled
I Can Dare To Be an Achiever
Keys to Healing Rejection
The Power of Forgiveness
The Power of the Blood
Receiving Resurrection Power
Renew Your Mind
Solving Life's Problems
Speak the Word
Standing in the Gap
The Story of Esther
Tithes • Offerings • Alms • God's Plan for Blessing You
Winning Over Weight
Women of the Word